To Harvey

from

(signature)

GOD, MONEY, AND YOU

GOD MONEY AND YOU

GEORGE OTIS

FLEMING H. REVELL COMPANY

OLD TAPPAN, NEW JERSEY

*To Mary Walker, from whose hours of
Bible research and prayer, the fabric
of this book was woven.*

and

*To Robert Pymm whose able work
opened the opportunity to do this book.*

CONTENTS

PREFACE

It is a day of paper gold, computer credit, puts and calls, and all-purpose credit cards and special drawing rights. A strange hour when experts applaud as the dollar plummets.

This is the day of the ten-nation monetary confederation and experiments with a new checkless-cashless system. Now that all have social security numbers, could this prove to be a dry run for that *mark* of the approaching tribulation? It would make a perfect system to control all buying and selling, wouldn't it?

Yes, it's a foreboding hour, as violent winds whip across the world's fragile economic networks. God's children must be alert as never before to these important forces. They've all been foretold in the Bible and we must now be sharply tuned to God's Word.

Before I ever became a Christian, twenty long and intense years were spent in what some call big business. These were action-packed years made up of both failures and successes—a long and exciting economics course. Many valuable lessons were learned from successful business leaders. But at times the way was lonely and hard. Those formative years etched strong impressions.

After the day I met the Lord and my new life of High Adventure began, I faced up to a new challenge. Reconciling life in the shop with that in the prayer room was rugged for me. Could it be done? Would it ever work? There were many new questions swirling. Aren't some of God's laws unworkable and even irrelevant in this twentieth century?

Should we sell the Cadillac? Can I take those customers to parties and nightclubs? If God made man the head, then why do women control so much of the wealth? And why do so many Christians live in continual financial shambles? Etc., etc., etc.

Being an inquisitive type, I wanted answers from someone on how to function on this unfamiliar Christian plateau. I thought, surely someone has written a book on the Christian and money that will help me make the transition. But I couldn't find it and set

9

off through my new world alternately messing things up and slowly learning from the marvelous Guidebook clutched in my hand.

I'm still learning and I haven't graduated, but I want to share the God and Money treasures that I have discovered in my fifteen years of High Adventure with Jesus.

I've found that there are millions of dedicated Christians who are also struggling with facets of Christian finances. Each trying to live a testimony in this trying, tempting, complicated and emotional area of money.

There are myriad daily choices in the nitty-gritty realities of business. Is the Bible inflexible or adjustable to such a time? They say, "Everyone does it anymore." It's twentieth-century culture and new morality ethics versus that Book twenty times a day. Which will I choose?

Newsboys, housewives, businessmen, evangelists, politicians, students, lawyers, laborers, athletes and missionaries—none escape the relentless encounter with choices, choices, choices. The simple test: "What would Jesus do?"

Will God prosper me if I follow the Book? Can it still work in this jet age? The answer is a thundering YES!

GEORGE OTIS

GOD, MONEY, AND YOU

1

GOD'S TREASURE MAP

The course of life is run through a corridor of ever-varying winds and forces. Certain forces press relentlessly every day of man's life. Love, hate, sex, money. He feels the pressures, temptations, joys, and sorrows of some aspect of their workings from morning until night, and year after year. They interweave conscious and subconscious thought, fabricating a tapestry of his character.

His decisions and the course of his life are deeply influenced by them. They are highly emotional forces! Money is basically an expression of a man's productiveness.

From the day man himself shattered the face-to-face communion with God in bountifully-stocked Eden, his destiny has been to live "by the sweat of his brow." Since that serpent and sin, man has struggled to make his living by his own toil. Man chose that course when he disobeyed his loving God who had prepared an indescribably better life for him. When man earned the curse of his livelihood by that disobedience, he triggered a flawed relationship with God and nature. It set loose striving with the earth and the competitiveness with all creatures that we now experience.

After Eden, God had to restructure His dealing with man and set down rules and laws. But our Maker thoughtfully provided man a wonderful new handbook and operations manual. We call it the Bible—a 1,265-page love letter from God. Eight hundred and forty-six thousand vital and loving words written for you personally. Its perfect guidelines are fully in force today, and violations bring all the grief and heartache that persons and nations suffer. The Bible reveals the course of victory and it always has the last word. It doesn't ignore man—man ignores it.

God gave His rules to help us, not to deny us. He wants the very best for His children. When will we ever learn that God is on our side? Getting to know His laws and then applying them brings harmony and life success. It is vital that we look more closely and find how important and exciting they really are. We must learn how we can make these spiritual laws work for us.

God has so very much to say on this matter of money and finances.

He uses the pressures and disciplines of money, of making a living, and material security to shape and mold our spirit. These shaping, economic winds blow regularly and sometimes violently. Proper spiritual response to these forces can bring growth of character. Correct reactions accelerate the grooming of our own spirit for a fabulous eternity. Learning to harmonize with God's laws of economics will prosper us right now as well as prepare us for eternity.

On the other hand, careless responses to these forces can be destructive. Failure to react in the financial realm in accord with God's Word can bring real problems. It isn't a man's energetic pursuit of success in itself that is the problem. It was God Himself who said: "Replenish the earth and subdue it" Genesis, Chapter 1, and "And whatsoever ye do in word or deed, do all in the name of the Lord Jesus . . ." Colossians, Chapter 3. Certain of the heroes of the Bible were exceptionally wealthy men.

It is rather the violation of His Word in wealth-related matters that brings chaos and heartache. Coveting the fruits of another's work, cheating, lusting for riches, worrying over financial security, selfishness, laziness, etc.

It is this type of violation of spiritual laws that brings down those money-related woes. Money is a dominating factor in broken marriages. Money arguments break up friendships, businesses, and even churches. Money sets nation against nation. Money is behind robberies, violence, and murder. Even so, money itself isn't the root. It's the *lusting* for money that is evil. Those who have no money can and sometimes do lust for it as much as those who have a lot.

God can, however, use these strong life currents swirling around the money realm. He can orchestrate these to test, teach, and shape our spirit. This short life on earth is really a School of the Holy Ghost—a great spiritual laboratory.

During many real-life situations, we feel the interplay on our person of Satan's "unholy spirit" trying to urge us to cheat on God's Word (temptation). Simultaneously, we sense God's Holy Spirit and His Word prompting our soul to follow God's rules (conscience). There is a perpetual warring inside between Satan's ways and God's. It is on this great battleground of the soul that ultimate destiny is set for every man.

Through ten thousand tests and choices in one lifetime we are slowly etched into that image we choose by our own free will. Either we grow in spirit more and more beautiful like Jesus, or grow more and more ugly like the prince of this world. You can view it in the countenance of a godly person contrasted to that of the depraved evil one.

Do you see it? You, too, are being slowly molded—yes, *molded* —choice by choice, and decision by decision—shaped into the image of either one or the other. There is no middle ground. You are heading one way or the other toward darkness or light.

The forces of Jesus and of Satan can be felt contending for each life. But *we* have the power to choose. God gives each the will to select. If his choice is toward God's Kingdom, then He even supplies the power by the Holy Spirit to make good that course.

The powerful grind of finances affects every life. This is why God recorded in the Bible the myriad things related to money. He wants us to have His secrets of prosperity and peace. These are unseen by the world for they are not received by the children of darkness.

More than half my life was spent following my former "father," the prince of this world. Even so, few men, including myself, have given themselves over completely to the ways of this world. Rather, we each become a blend of some of God's principles and some of the lethal principles of God's adversary. Satan always manages to delude even his most evil subjects into feeling that they are really good people. It's the Robin Hood syndrome! Gangsters and Mafia members grandiosely distribute a little charity from their bags of stolen money. You know the story. . . .

My own life, while under that old banner, resulted in what the world would call success. But even while enjoying a financial statement reflecting at times a million, there was never a real joy or contentment. Just a feeling of incompleteness and a driving unnatural lust for still *more*. Even with a large bank account there can be the subconscious torment that it may be lost, and at stages mine would slip through my hands somehow. "Ye have sown much, and bring in little; ye eat, but ye have not enough; ye drink, but ye are not filled with drink; ye clothe you, but there is none warm; and he that earneth wages earneth wages to put it into a bag with holes" Haggai, Chapter 1.

When Satan has his ring in your nose he never leads you by the peaceful still waters. Only God's prosperity brings contentment and that deep soul-rest. Since that day I found Jesus, He has been teaching me a few things about reconciling life in the Spirit with my work. How to translate life in the cathedral to life in the shop.

Let's take a thrilling journey through that Book to discover some of God's success secrets. It can be life-enriching if you will come on this treasure hunt and then *apply* the sure coin we will dig. How good of Him to leave a *perfect* treasure map for us—the Bible. Now come all the way on our hunt. We'll be going over some terrain that isn't easy. In places we will at first seem to be off our treasure path. Others will hurt as tender spots are touched. Some depart from the rutted trails of tradition. But the Bible, God's Treasure Map, is perfect and it will lead us to a prosperous and peaceful highland that He has marked just for His own.

2

BEING SYNCHRONIZED WITH GOD'S CLOCK

Behind the darkness gathering over this planet there is a clock ticking. It is fearful for the unbelievers who lack understanding of the macabre events being played out. It is the last act on the stage of this dispensation. Its death rattle strikes fear into the heart of the spiritually blind, and rightfully so!

It is apparent to every creature that some great crescendo is looming. There is a polarization of light and darkness, of good and evil. It is urgent that every Christian be tuned to the Spirit of God, that he might interpret this kaleidoscope of events in the perspective of eternity. Only the spiritually sensitive can see through the disintegration of our age to the approaching Light in the distance.

Through spectacles of faith the Christian views not only the falling curtain of this sick age, but he senses the looming of a brand new age. Only the believer can penetrate this darkness. The Christian remembers that resurrection came only after the darkness of the cross. He has seen the empty tomb. And he has the benefit of God's Word which pictures the entire human pageant. The believer knows how this one ends. He has read the final act.

But let's take a hard look at this tired globe on which we hurtle through space. Every condition on her breathes climax! Every chart and graph is streaking toward finale. She teems with four billion people who multiply to choke her cities and plains. Her streams flow with poison and her air is a deadly yellow. One third of her passengers hunger as the lands groan to feed her hordes. The cities blow their straining power turbines and the pipes begin to trickle because of her diminishing water sheds. Even the fish of her seas are depleted. All nature groans and travails. . . .

Venereal diseases rage through masses. Foul breezes have spawned a tornado! Bikini to mini-skirt to *Playboy* magazine to

lewd movies to wife-swapping to topless bars to live sex on stage
to sex orgies to devastated homes to hollow-eyed, weeping children. Hail the new morality!

We watch in sick fascination as the intricate world monetary
systems convulse. The delicate web of international commerce
and finances vibrates toward collapse.

The pulse of war has increased her rhythm. In recent decades
men were shocked and grieved as lesser battles began to flame
every twenty or thirty years. Now the horsemen of war gallop
at incredible speed through the earth. First to the east, then west.
Then to the north. Then south. Where will the cruel fires break
out next? In the last days "Wars and rumors of wars . . ." God
said, Matthew, Chapter 24 (RSV).

And He said men's hearts would be failing them for fear. Now
bombs scaled in MEGATONS! Missiles and aircraft faster than
sound. Crime, immorality, hate—all spin before our eyes. Greed
and sensual appetites predominate. The voices of righteousness
and reason are mocked in the United Nations. Delegates scream
and cheer as the nation that slaughtered a million Christians is
welcomed. In this present madness men and women blur vision
with liquor and pull the shades of reality with dope. Iniquity
covers the earth. . . .

Yes, we orbit together on a sick, convulsing planet!

One important day Jesus scolded those standing around Him.
He said to them in effect, "You look up at the sky to tell what
the weather is going to be tomorrow." Then He uttered a burst
of exhortation that flashes down the corridor of time to explode
at the feet of our generation. Jesus wanted His own to be syn-
chronized with the Father's spiritual clock.

Jesus said we should observe all things about us that can
reveal what's about to happen in the spiritual realm. It's in the
spiritual realm that all things develop before manifestation in the
natural realm. Jesus knew that our generation in particular would
need to know the spiritual time. He said, "O ye hypocrites, ye
can discern the face of the sky; but can ye not discern the signs
of the times" Matthew, Chapter 16? The Bible is our clock.

The age-closing signs in the seventies are so vivid that only

*the dead are blind to them. We stand on the threshold of the most
electrifying minute in human history . . . Christ's return for
His own!*

Jesus said no man would know the exact hour of His return.
He did, however, reveal in crystalline detail the worldwide circumstances that would prevail just prior to it. He wanted every
believer to know when that moment was approaching. Never
before has there been a generation that this "shoe of God" fit.
One of the last key prophecies has now been fulfilled. The Jews
have in our own lifetime returned to their ancient homeland.

The Lord said that in the last days there would be great distress
and perplexity. He said there would be a great increase in law-
lessness. Today, riots, police killings, robbery, murder, bombings,
rape, and sabotage punctuate our life.

And He said, "Go to now, ye rich men, weep and howl for your
miseries that shall come upon you. Your riches are corrupted . . .
Your gold and silver is cankered; and the rust of them shall be a
witness against you, and shall eat your flesh as it were fire. Ye have
heaped treasure together for the last days" James, Chapter 5.

It's an hour to spend for Christ, not a time to hoard. A time
to invest for eternity, not a time to hug the withering coins of
time for God also said: "But as the days of Noe were, so shall
also the coming of the Son of Man be. For as in the days that
were before the flood they were eating and drinking, marrying
and giving in marriage, until the day that Noe entered into the
ark, and knew not until the flood came, and took them all away;
so shall also the coming of Son of Man be" Matthew, Chapter 24.

"This know also, that in the last days perilous times shall come.
For men shall be lovers of their own selves, covetous, boasters,
proud, blasphemers, disobedient to parents, unthankful, unholy,
without natural affection, truce-breakers, false accusers, incon-
tinent, fierce, despisers of those that are good, traitors, heady,
highminded, lovers of pleasures more than lovers of God; having
a form of godliness, but denying the power thereof . . ." 2 Timothy, Chapter 3.

And Jesus said, "When ye see these things come to pass, know
ye that the kingdom of God is nigh at hand" Luke, Chapter 21.

And now—the age-crowning event that we shall experience soon! A beautiful *Sonburst* heralding our arriving King! "For the Lord himself shall descend from heaven with a shout, with the voice of the archangel, and with the trump of God: and the dead in Christ shall rise first: Then we which are alive and remain shall be caught up together with them in the clouds, to meet the Lord in the air: and so shall we ever be with the Lord" 1 Thessalonians, Chapter 4.

The Bible is nearly one quarter prophecy, with hundreds of verses foretelling future events. Some 90 percent of these Godly proclamations have already passed from Bible prophecy into the pages of our history books. Each has taken place exactly how and precisely when God said it would. We can be certain that the remaining events prophesied shall take place right on schedule.

According to God's own Word His clock will now strike twelve! Are you ready? Are you really? It must grieve God to hear so many of His own down here glibly mouthing, "These are the end-time days" and "Jesus is coming soon."

You say, "How could that bother Him?" Here's how!

Many of us repeat "Jesus is coming" then prove with our actions that we don't really believe it. It's a time to review all our priorities. If we are about to face Christ, then our life-style, holdings, schedules, plans, programs and spending bear reworking.

If we really believe He is coming back during our lifetime then why do we struggle over our wills and buy insurance so that our children can benefit in the *next generation?* Will there be a next generation as we know it? Are God's words to be trusted or not?

I think it was in May of last year that I was invited to speak in central Oregon. The auditorium of the beautiful old church was filled on a rainy Sunday night. The message God had for me that evening was along these very lines.

The Holy Spirit seemed to be moving to encourage some people present to act *now* in their giving to His work, before it was past their hour. This particular church is really moving for God, and the shortage of seats for those hungry for God was evident that night. Some had to stand.

Toward the end of the message I was moved to ask every person to ask God what He wanted them to do about money and holdings beyond their actual needs. They were to pray for guidance and courage to give that night, in order that the revival might grow.

Fifteen minutes after the closing prayer a lady knocked at the pastor's study. God had spoken to her. She knew that she was to act immediately on something that had been stirring inside her for a year. The pastor's eyes were moist as he heard her, under an annointing of God's Spirit, give a large parcel of oil-producing land. It was to be sold to build the urgently needed sanctuary addition. She was ecstatic with joy and relief at her obedience. She was transferring her treasure up where moth and rust couldn't erode it. You can imagine the thrill that was mine to witness this act of generous giving.

Recently, I had the privilege of returning to this same church. One of my first questions to the assistant pastor as I was picked up at the airport was about the progress on their new building. When he told me they still weren't quite funded I was shocked. "What about that oil property gift?" I inquired, "That was enough to pay for the whole project."

Then he shared what happened after I had left. Early in the week following the service this lady had gone to see her lawyer to execute transfer of the deed to the church. Her lawyer, who was not a Christian, stalled her in his blind efforts to be helpful. (If you don't have a Christian lawyer, follow his advice on legal but not on spiritual matters.)

He immediately phoned her heirs (who were also his clients) to suggest that they ask her to take a few weeks to think this through. He wanted her to be sure she hadn't acted on some emotional impulse that she would later regret. She hadn't objected when the lawyer asked her permission to review the gifting with her heirs.

When both her beloved children and also the lawyer pressed her for further deliberation, she agreed to the reasonable-sounding advice. She delayed the signing of the deed transfer papers even though God had told her to do it. She had said yes to Him, but now hesitated.

Three weeks and two days after my meeting this wonderful Christian lady she suddenly died. Inheritance taxes and her unbelieving relatives got that which was meant to fuel that Oregon revival. She was utterly robbed of her blessing and so was the work of the Kingdom.

A friend recently said to me, "You know, my grandfather also thought Christ was coming back while he was alive, so I just don't know." I said, "Don't be deceived. Your grandfather sounds like a splendid man, but Christ couldn't have come back in his day. All of the end-time prophecies hadn't yet been fulfilled. God foretold that the Jews would be scattered through the earth, and then in the last days miraculously regathered into their land. He couldn't have come in your grandfather's day because this hadn't happened yet." Do you see it? The Lord said there would be such scoffers about His return at the very end. We mustn't be like the careless virgins that saw the Bridegroom's door shut right in their faces.

Yes, many cry, "He's coming soon!" but they act as though all things will continue as from the beginning. How terrifying to think of missing Christ's return by a few hours like those poor virgins. How would you like to contemplate this through eternity from the wrong side of that door?

We're still pulling down our barns and building bigger ones. We are buying new homes, working out our old-age security and constructing church buildings to last a hundred years. We are buying two cars when one would do and shopping for a bigger TV. We rationalize these as "necessities" while the missionary and evangelist falter for lack of funds!

Do we really believe He is coming soon? Christians hold assets valued at billions of dollars. Yes, I said *billions!* Businesses, lands, stocks, jewelry, properties, cars, boats, bonds, mortgages and money, beyond what is needed to hold us until this age abruptly ends.

What are we doing anyway? Are we storing these for the Antichrist's use during the tribulation? If we really believe our Bible, shouldn't we get "our bags packed" to go with Jesus? Shouldn't we shift our practice of giving the Lord's work 10 percent of our *income* and start giving also from our *capital?* Let's begin to sell off all but the essentials and trim down for our trip of trips. The proceeds from this "moving time" liquidation can suddenly release enough to the Lord's workers to finish in *a year or two* the spreading of the gospel. ". . . And then shall the end come" Matthew, Chapter 24. Praise God! Let's do it!

Then, too, it grieves the Lord for us to hypocritically make the kind of last will and testament that has become commonplace in the Christian family. Sometimes a Christian will enter into a will arrangement so that at his death the residue of his estate goes to XYZ church or ABC missionary organization. He then sits back and lets his heart coo, "I have done a good thing. The Lord must surely rejoice in me today for I have left Him everything in my will." It's different for our particular generation.

How sad if he thinks that's all he should do. An honest examination would reveal that nothing perfect has been accomplished by that will, for this Christian has actually said, "Dear Lord, I want to give you everything—after I'm dead and can't use it anymore." Do you see it? God doesn't look on the substance of the gift. God isn't poor, you know. He looks upon the heart. What is it then? Sure, make that will in case of some emergency, but start giving of your substance here.

Yes, we should do our giving now! Give to Him now when we could still use it, but enjoy still more sharing it with Him. This is the best way to transfer our gold into heaven where those moths and that rust cannot eat it up. Let's do it now! NOW! NOW!

We should also reexamine our heart on such things as giving only where tax credit is available. How does that look to God? Oh, those tricky hearts!

Prayerfully consult the Lord as to all the changes that should now be made in your life, then pray for the wisdom and the courage to put into action preparations for *that trip!*

3

THE PLASTIC BOMB

Christians, too, can fall into the trap of idolizing things. They aren't immune to that costly game "keeping up with the Joneses."

Jim and Rhoda parked their Lincoln and rang our doorbell one night last year. It was troubling to see the look on their faces. Rhoda's expensive grooming didn't hide how she had aged.

She spoke first, "Jim and I are separating. We just can't take it any more. . . ." Virginia brought coffee, then after a few niceties Jim and then Rhoda sketched in for us the details of their crisis.

They had met at Bible school. They were married graduation day and Jim had taken a job at McDonnell Douglas near where they had bought a little house. Within three years Becky and Mark had come along and they were walking with the Lord as a young family. Rhoda's high-school friend had married Carl Stern, a stockbroker, and they made frequent visits to the Sterns' plush Brentwood home. Rhoda began to grow ashamed of their own place, and they eventually made an offer on a house in a wealthy neighborhood.

This move created chain-reaction pressures for better furniture, clothes and a new car. Slowly they accumulated credit cards of one kind and another. Both Jim's employment and financial records were good. The bills began to mount and Rhoda started to complain about Jim's paycheck. More than one of their spats included Rhoda's jabs about the Sterns' prosperity.

Along with the financial pressures there began to develop a coolness toward the Lord. It was subtle, but it grew until first the Wednesday night prayer meetings were dropped, and later the Sunday night meetings. Finally they were going to church on intermittent Sunday mornings—especially after they got a new camper. After a year the overwhelming bills spurred Rhoda to think about going to work. Somehow it never occurred to her to reorganize expenditures to match Jim's adequate paycheck. The idol of possessions had crept into both of their hearts.

Rhoda's decision to hunt for a job generated more friction. Jim had failed in all this too, since he had slowly relinquished his role under God as boss of their marriage. Jim allowed his weakening leadership to develop in the guise of love for Rhoda and a desire for harmony. It never works. It is cowardly, and the opposite of real love.

Rhoda finally went to work in Sears' accounting department. At first this seemed to be helping, but soon she had to have better clothes and another car for the new job. She began to succumb to a growing appetite for more furniture. Meanwhile, the day-care for the children was expensive, and both kids were starting to get into trouble. Then came a blowup at tax time. Both had forgotten how their combined income would balloon taxes.

Throughout recent years both Rhoda and Jim had gotten the credit-card disease. The cards were so nice to use. At times of discouragement they would use their little plastic cards for a trip, to eat out, or to buy clothes.

Harmony in the house was decreasing in proportion to the financial disintegration. Now they seemed to be yelling and accusing each other daily. Here it was again: "Ye have sown much, and bring in little; ye eat, but ye have not enough; ye drink, but ye are not filled with drink; ye clothe you, but there is none warm; and he that earneth wages earneth wages to put into a bag with holes" Haggai, Chapter 1. Now joy in their things was minimal. There wasn't prayer in the home any more and it still hadn't dawned on them to adjust that spending. They were marching mindlessly to a fool's tune . . . just hoping something would work out without having to change anything.

With growing "warfare" at home the enemy began to move in on the opportunity they had opened. First Jim, then Rhoda, started to flirt with someone at work. Those all-purpose cards had bought them trouble, and their easy-credit Lincoln had transported two miserable people to our door.

It's almost as if those little white cards were invented in hell. God says, "Owe no one anything . . ." Romans, Chapter 13. Credit cards fuel our temptation to buy things we don't need and haven't yet earned. Much of today's credit comes with extremely costly charges built in. When fully analyzed, they usually amount to 12 to 20 percent!

Some Christians need to destroy those credit cards in their pockets, as they can, for some like Jim and Rhoda, be time bombs to shatter happiness and peace. There is a valuable automatic discipline built in when we have to pay out cash for something we want. Do you have the courage to cut up yours? It could be one of the smartest things you ever clipped. It could mean as much this year as clipping coupons.

Generous husbands thoughtlessly give them to wives, some of whom are overly tempted by their magic. Every divorce court and marriage counselor will testify that easy credit is helping to wreck countless marriages. Credit cards do have a place in business where accounting is aided, but they are frequently an expensive threat to an individual. Even some businesses are abandoning them as too costly and too much of an expense ballooner.

But Jim and Rhoda were finally desperate enough to pray and seek help. After those cross accusations and a time of prayer they submitted to stern exhortation. Before that evening was over they were changing. They asked forgiveness from each other and from the Lord. After all, it was God's Word they had violated. They promised to destroy their own credit cards when they got home. They also decided to sell their luxurious home, the camper and the Lincoln.

Yes, they had sinned against God, and as they slowly lost fellowship with Him they became increasingly vulnerable to an appetite for "things."

But when they finally turned to God in the throes of crisis, He healed this sickness. And when they started to do all they could in their finances He seemed to start stretching their income. It was a little like the widow's supply of meal. Within fifteen months their bills were current even though Rhoda had quit working at Sears.

Not only was their marriage restored, but they are now active again in church and a home prayer group.

Jim and Rhoda's broken fellowship with God had started to erode communion with one another. A great marriage must be

based on our great God. The most vibrant marriages are ones
where both mates are fervent for Christ. From Him flows the
romantic energy for a real love affair in the home.

Divorce is almost a death in one's relationship to God. No
marriage crisis is ever impossible for Him to restore and He will
even make it better than new. That's hard to believe, isn't it?
But God didn't say "Once love is dead it's always dead." That's
from the pen of a little man. God is the author and the source
of all real love. One word from Him will heal and renew. It's a
small thing for Him to give a sincere Christian who has lost love
for a mate a new divine implant of love. We have seen Him do
it many times. He can restore love to a dimension that exceeds that
of the bruised couple's courting days. We know of what we speak,
for He has done it in our own marriage!

God has shown us how profound human marriage really is.
Marriage was designed by Him to provide joy, help, companion-
ship and ecstasy while on earth. But it is still more. . . .

Your marriage is a great laboratory. It is a place of test-
ing the development for your *ultimate marriage relationship.*
Christ is observing every aspect of your behavior in this earthly
marriage. He has a vital interest in your qualities as a mate. Are
you faithful? Are you affectionate? Are you disciplined? Do you
fail in the heat of adversity? Will you quit on your earthly mate?

You see, He wants to know your quality *before He takes you
as His mate!* Do you see it? You dare not quit in your marriage!
He wants your marriage to be magnificent in every department
and will always help.

Let the Holy Spirit develop in your marriage laboratory
the kind of fragrance that He desires in you. The more difficult
your own marriage challenge, the more fragrant you can become
to Him. Remember that the sweetest aroma is from the crushed
rose.

I can't appreciate the whimpering one who comes for help saying, "I've been praying for the strength to be able to tolerate my
husband. You just don't know how hard my life is. Pray that I'll
have the strength to stand him!"

Jesus doesn't prize a martyr as His bride. He wants a lover. We
say to them, "Stop praying for strength to tolerate, but for a blazing

new love, affection and patience." Yes, for both! Some gag as they first try to pray this way. It's very difficult to force these words from their mouths. They find it so hard to believe God can do it for them.

But it's fabulous how many times we have seen it work. Our God loves to work miracles! It is He who shouts "Is anything too hard for the Lord" Genesis, Chapter 8 (RSV)?

Oh, how God loves to work in "impossible" situations!

4

....

SANTA AND THE BUNNY

....

The most important event for man since Creation was that astounding day God the Father sent down the most valuable gift in all of His universe. Imagine the Owner of all that ever was and is and ever shall be delivering His supreme treasure—His very Son. The anniversary of that titanic event named Christmas is indeed worth joyous, noble celebration!

Many Christians now feel a growing repulsion each succeeding Christmas season at the blasphemy of its celebration. How like the prince of this world to pervert this supreme anniversary! Since he couldn't stop men from celebrating, he began to distort. This distortion has brought about some grotesque aspects to this Number One Event. For example, imagine how God's heart must be repelled by the introduction of a fat red-suited fraud to syphon off the love of the little children Christ so adored. Now bear with me. . . .

It's no longer the anticipation of Christ's birthday we await so eagerly. A birthday is a time when gifts are to be carried to the one whose birth date it is. Look at the Bible pattern on that first Christmas. Guided by God's Spirit they came bearing gifts *to* Christ. Today His person is nearly obliterated in the raucous stampede at the shopping centers. His gentle voice buried in the honking holiday traffic, and the drunken cocktail-party squeals.

Hardly are the gifts for Christ anymore, but for *each other*. It is remindful of the kind of gift giving foretold in Revelation that will take place during the tribulation as the slaying of God's prophets is celebrated. The present Christmas tradition hardly includes giving from grateful creatures to their magnificent Lord. We have lost our Christmas perspective in a hundred ways.

Have you felt that strange emptiness after opening the last package under the tree? It's partly the insatiable appetite of our human senses never satisfied with temporal things.

29

Only things of the Spirit are lasting and soul-satisfying. Wesley caught the fragrance of eternal Christmas with this burst of inspiration:

> Christ, by highest heaven adored,
> Christ, the everlasting Lord:
> Late in time, behold Him come,
> Offspring of a virgin's womb.
> Veiled in flesh and Godhead see,
> Hail th' incarnate Deity!
> Pleased as man with men to appear
> Jesus our Immanuel here.
>
> Hail, the heav'n born Prince of Peace!
> Hail, the Sun of righteousness!
> Light and life to all He brings,
> Ris'n with healing in His wings.
> Mild He lays His glory by
> Born that man no more may die;
> Born to raise the sons of earth;
> Born to give them second birth.
>
> Come, desire of nations, come!
> Fix in us Thy humble home:
> Rise, the woman's conqu'ring seed,
> Bruise in us the serpent's head,
> Adam's likeness now efface,
> Stamp Thine image in its place:
> Second Adam from above,
> Reinstate us in Thy love.
>
> Hark! the herald angels sing,
> Glory to the newborn King.

Let's unfrock forever that red-suited lie named SANTA. Even the letters of his name rearranged spell SATAN. The hoax is more than a little deadly to the spirit of the child. Do you remember that moment as a child when it suddenly struck you that this whole Santa business was a fabrication? I do.

This revelation that Santa is fantasy can inflict a deep scar—
a foundation for doubt. Satan has built this trap, and we've co-
operated. The young mind wonders if Jesus may also be a fraud—
fantasy—folklore! Thus Jesus often moves along with Santa into
the realm of the question mark.

Then there is the sheer burden of giving—because it's expected.
Frantically struggling and shopping for gifts that aren't given to
honor Him. Many given out of duty . . . caught up in a great
mill of tradition that has lost its original meaning. Have you
sensed the mingling of joy and heaviness that makes up your
mood during the holiday time? I am convinced that the Holy Spirit
Himself is working on believers trying to bring perspective back
to the heart.

And such debts are built up during this time! Saturation ad-
vertising along with easy credit and seven-day shopping have
made it so enticing to overspend. That, coupled with fear that
we might be embarrassed by not giving enough to some person,
revs up the wheels of commerce. Billions are spent to satisfy a
tradition of men that grieves God's heart. Christ is often neglected,
ignored, and man's spirit abused during the very season of Christ's
birth. Prayer has been blasted from the schoolroom and now
the honoring of Christ's birthday has come under fire in schools.

I have also shuddered in recent years as I have seen evangelism
terminated in some churches to accommodate holiday routines.
No, I've also felt my own spiritual thermometer helplessly fall from
the hectic holiday busyness. Christ longs for the gift of our love
and worship toward Him, and Christmas should be our highest
hour of thanksgiving.

You know, it excites me to think of the thousands that could
be brought into His Kingdom if we Christians would modify our
own Christmas-spending orgy. What if this year we were to flow
that same silver and gold into the Lord's work instead?

Let's pray for the courage to break these Satanic shackles per-
verting the anniversary of Christ's birth, and purpose in our
hearts to channel our love and our giving to the Lord *this
Christmas!*

The only other day to match Christmas in spiritual magnificence
is the anniversary of Christ rising from the grave—Easter. Just

think of it . . . Satan has taken his best shot at the Son of God.
He has engineered and then watched Christ's destruction on the
cross. You can almost sense the wild celebrations held that day
throughout Satan's spiritual domain.

Satan's ultimate strategy down through the ages had been to
cut off the seed of the woman to avoid the bruising of his own
head, as foretold by God Himself. Now he had finally done it out
on that cross on Calvary's slope. The rusted spikes were drawn
and the dead frame of Jesus was pulled loose. His cold body was
wound with cloths and He was sealed into a rock cave forever.
Then set in on the earth three long days of eerie quiet. . . .

Suddenly a message of terror raced through the communica-
tions channels of the fallen spirit world. Christ is preaching in
hell! He has risen! He's out! He's loose! He lives!

That moment tipped the destiny of mankind. Satan, the victor,
withered to Satan, the vanquished! Look at the picture of Satan
that God reveals in Isaiah's prophecy. When finally seen he will be
a surprise to God's children. Here's mighty Lucifer in the state to
which Easter has reduced him: "They that see thee shall nar-
rowly look upon thee, and consider thee, saying, Is this the man
that made the earth to tremble, that did shake kingdoms . . ."
Isaiah, Chapter 14?

Yes, our many-splendored Easter! Anniversary of the day everlasting life for us burst from the grave! But the old serpent is
still slithering to tarnish Christ's work. Still fouling the lilies. The
motor of the abominable Easter bunny with his basket of phony
eggs has been wound up by Satan and set loose across the human
stage to steal the resurrection.

Why? To pervert the day—to confuse the children and to hide
the empty tomb!

When will we Christians through love of God stop falling in
step with that bunny and Santa? Those Easter eggs may even be
traceable to the ancient fertility rites so abhorrent to the Lord.
And our bunny has gained new fame in Hugh Heffner's *Playboy*.
Farfetched, you say? We shouldn't be naive spiritually "Know
your enemy," is the first precept of warfare. *You* are both the
battleground and the prize.

We must teach our children the wonder, beauty and significance
of Easter. Resist the confusion from that bunny and egg. Have

the courage to break these chains of distortion and blasphemous traditions.

Can we, for Jesus' sake turn these noblest of anniversaries, Christmas and Easter, back to Him? We now have a golden chance to complete the spreading of the gospel instead of filling the pockets of some ungodly merchants. Let's worship the Lord this season with funds we have been misspending.

Yes, it thrills me! Do you see our chance to turn that which Satan meant for ill to God's glory? Try to visualize the impact from the sudden flooding of tens of millions of dollars for reaching the last of the untold. We can speed up Christ's return by this, for He said, "And this gospel of the kingdom shall be preached in all the world . . . and then shall the end come" Matthew, Chapter 24.

That poorly equipped band of early Christians shook the gates of hell as they cast their everything into the coffers to get the job done. And they turned the world upside down.

Just look at what we now have to finish the job—things that Paul never had. High speed printing presses, radio, television, telephones, Bibles, trains, cars and jets!

Nearly every spot on earth is reachable within hours by missionaries and evangelists who are even now standing ready except for the needed money. Every place on our globe is reachable by radio and Christian literature today. All or portions of the Bible have now been translated into most languages. The Great Gospel Machine is now ready to move . . . it has lacked only the fuel of finances to roll at full throttle. Let's give Jesus the biggest gift ever. Let's pour treasures at His feet this year. Let's bring back the King!

5

SPIRITUAL EFFICIENCY

Have you ever wondered why the lives of some like Billy Graham, Katherine Kuhlman, David Wilkerson and others seem to have the impact of a thousand other people? A careful examination is rewarding. Their ministries demonstrate the extraordinary impact a single life can have when God's principles plus faith are applied. The mark on humanity and the productivity of Paul's life further illustrate this potential. It is attainable by *any* Christian who will pay the price, for God is no respecter of persons.

But certain of God's laws and principles will also work in the natural realm for anyone who applies them. Isn't that a shocker? Unbelievers never realize that much of their effectiveness is due to application of God's principles. The lives of Ford, Carnegie, Edison, Steinmetz, Isaac Watts and DaVinci were incredibly prolific. God's laws of nature, productivity, resourcefulness and integrity work for any men who apply them. Thus, we see that many unbelievers benefit by the godly laws that He has set into the earth. The rain falls on both the just and the unjust.

But wealth and fame don't equate happiness. The ungodly man may achieve material prosperity apart from God, but he can never achieve soul satisfaction. Riches gained apart from God are a snare and they bring little peace, " . . . For a man's life consisteth not in the abundance of the things which he possesseth" Luke, Chapter 12.

Concerning success apart from God, it has been said: "Show me a *self*-made man and I will show you a failure in life." The world's poets throw a glamorous aura on the self-made man, but since *self*-sufficiency is at enmity with God's way you find heartache and emptiness in the bosom of such. This may be why the suicide rate is found to be higher among the wealthy. But God says His children can learn certain things from the wisdom of this

34

world. ". . . for the children of this world are in their generation wiser than the children of light" Luke, Chapter 16. Let's browse through a few of the secrets of extraordinary lives. . . .

TIME

The successful have invariably learned the stewardship of time. It is our most squandered treasure. It is strictly metered to each. It's what men do with their allotment that counts. If only Christians could see its precious nature. It is our premier resource.

The successful executive has a keen sense of time. He employs elaborate measures to make time work for him instead of against him. He will be highly conscious as to the amount of time that he will allot to each appointment. He will not allow a visitor to ramble or waste his time.

Contrast this with the foolish person. Many sit night after night blank-faced before a television set viewing fables—unreality. It is like a narcotic that robs them of the precious components of life. Even as they watch, the time relentlessly ebbs away—tick, tick, tick. . . .

The effective man will balance his life between work, rest and recreation. The time-foolish man will choose an imbalance of pleasure and ease. He will be a clock-watcher on his job, counting the minutes until he can coast again. He will be in a camper racing for the lake, or with his ear bent to a ball game, while the effective man is working, studying, and producing. . . . ". . . lovers of pleasures more than lovers of God" 2 Timothy, Chapter 3.

The failure will grumble. He will often dislike work, dislike thinking, and hate to compete. He will criticize his boss and be the first to strike for less work at higher pay.

The believer can't get away with squandering time either. God doesn't prosper the Christians who will pray diligently for prosperity and then sit in their rocking chairs waiting for God to deliver it.

DISCIPLINE

Success requires disciplines that are sometimes painful. Discipline overcomes and prevails against our selfish desires. It requires doing a thing when we don't feel like it, and resisting the pull of our flesh.

This applies also to our prayers, praise and Bible study. The disciplined Christian does these even when he doesn't *feel* like it. God says that we should give Him a sacrifice of praise. That means to praise God even when we don't feel like it. Praise Him when we feel farthest from Him. That's a sacrifice. The times we feel farthest from God are exactly when it is most profitable to seek Him. God honors sacrifice and discipline. Discipline can bring harmony with God's laws and make them work for Him.

The fruits of discipline may be seen in the making of an athlete. A football star will practice nearly to the point of exhaustion. He, too, may want to be home watching television or sleeping, but instead will require himself to perfect his skills. After hours of practice he may force himself to run wind sprints. We oftentimes see a man with lesser natural attributes succeed over the gifted man. This can be accomplished in most realms when we pray for discipline and success motivation. If we lack this motivation we can pray for it. Make His desires our desires.

Most millionaires have paid a great price of courage, discipline, desire and hard work, all focused on their goal of achievement. Frequently the millionaire has fewer natural talents than many of those slouching in front of the tube.

THE EDGE

A successful man has learned to activate more of his magnificent God-designed mind. Science reveals that we utilize only some 5 percent of the incredible supercomputer called the brain. The effective man uses this for reasoning, logic, creativity, analysis and decisiveness. He has learned how to draw more productive thinking from it.

A Christian can have a significant advantage over others in gaining a fuller yield from his mind. This is why we see many brilliant Christian businessmen, writers, inventors, mathematicians, scientists, teachers, astronauts, athletes, pilots and engineers.

Harmony with their Creator brings the peace of mind and mental climate that's more conducive to precision thinking and superior decision-making. The mind functions more effectively when free from strains and clutter. The mind also benefits when it is coupled to a healthy body and a serene spirit. Here the Christian has a real edge. His heritage is the very mind of Christ as promised in the Word.

The unbeliever more frequently abuses his body and mind with worry, alcohol, carousing or other sins. Both the mind and the physiological system deteriorate with this abuse.

Ungodly men with their extra hangups and guilt complexes have more brain-clutter. The unbeliever doesn't have access to the cleansing power of the blood. Forgiveness of sin is no small advantage for the Christian businessman. His access to instant restoration of harmony with his Creator allows him to retain that peace of mind so conducive to keen thinking. That super cleansing agent—the blood of Jesus—has a brightening effect on the mind of a Christian and keeps it free from mind-fouling tensions.

I might inject here that even Christian minds, because of the Fall, still don't perform up to their designed level. Many of us are too proud to admit to imperfect memory. Most good executives know they can lose good ideas or forget appointments unless they write them down. I know my own limitations and it has greatly helped my productiveness to always carry a pad with me. You never know when an idea will come. I also keep a running listing of unfinished things and strike them out when done.

Then, isn't it wonderful that we have a God who has the ability to forget? He says that He remembers our confessed sins no more. This is His way of describing what is to me one of His most surprising and wonderful attributes. He wants us to learn to do likewise once He has forgiven us. The accuser of the brethren tries to negate this Christian advantage by getting us to dredge up and fret over sins God has forgotten. God wants us to erase our memory of them just as He has erased them from all heavenly records.

Meanwhile, the unbeliever has to live with his unforgiven sins. As they pile up one upon another they clutter his mind and foul his emotions. This causes him to struggle to operate efficiently because of his growing garbage pile. Can you see how he carries a handicap over the Christian? No wonder those psychiatrists' couches are never cold. The unbelievers rush in to find relief from hangups, but most psychiatrists can only wallpaper them over temporarily. Many try in vain to teach the distressed to live with

their sins and stresses. How superior is Christ's way! He elimi-
nates the sins forever, and then repairs their damage. Peace and
vitality return to the mind.

GOOD GUYS FINISH FIRST

The productiveness lost by unbelievers from alcohol and immorality is staggering. We see the ugly footprints across the Monday absentee records. The believer, with his efficiently operating
body and mind has an awesome advantage over people who "live
it up." You never find a man who sustains success after he begins
to drink excessively. Liquor and pills sap energy from the body,
mind and spirit, in a cruel, relentless way. That's why good
guys still finish first in business and in life. It's a statistical fact,
in spite of what the liquor commercials try to portray.

Control of fear is another powerful advantage for the Christian.
Fear is one of Satan's most used tools. It comes in many forms.
Fear stifles the delicate creative network of the mind. Fear is the
opposite of faith and is a destructive force. The Christian's edge
is peace that passes understanding. Worry is a spoiler. Faith and
confidence in God's supply and protection is a lubricant for the
mind. How wonderful that the Christian in a moment of fear
can "place a call" to his God for protection and for direction.
Then too, only the Christian can have the very "mind of Christ"
for all situations.

The ungodly are devastated by fears today! It is the hour
when God said men's hearts would be failing them for fear. Mental institutions are bulging with those afflicted from mind-blowing
fears. What a contrast with the Christian's peace of God! The
kind of peace that came to the disciples when they called on
Jesus to still the killer storm. How wonderful for the Christian
who can hide in the cleft of the Rock, Christ Jesus, while everything is shaken about him. Only he can know that soul-rest under
the shadow of God's wing. Christ is more than a security blanket!
He's for real.

This Prince of Peace provides our gyroscope in a reeling
world. The Christian can still think clearly when things are tough.
He looks his best in time of crisis. He knows that the One who

clothes the lilies of the field will provide for him tomorrow, even if the worst happens today.

Even so, the Christian must be on guard against Satan's fiery darts of fears and doubts. More than a few experience a great deal of self-doubt at times. One may become especially vulnerable when numerous failures and problems pile up. It may also be triggered by criticism from another believer! We face occasions like the one the old prophet described when the heavens seemed like brass.

Satan will go to work on the minds of the unwary and try to bring on a spirit of depression. You and I have felt it working on us. You will begin doubting yourself. Suddenly it seems like you can't do anything well. You feel as though your whole life has been so worthless. You don't like the way you look, think or act. Everything seems so hard and gloomy. Nobody seems to love you.

You've felt those attacks. You start to wonder what dreadful thing will happen to you next. God doesn't answer your prayers anymore, and you know it's all your fault. Your faith drains out and a mixture of hopelessness and gloom flows in.

It is imperative we take authority over such assaults. The Bible tells us that whenever the enemy comes in like a flood He will set up a standard against him. The blood-won victory banner of Jesus is that stopper!

When these defeatist darts start to come—don't receive them! Say "I know this is not of God. Fear is from the pit. I know I am weak, but Jesus is strong. He hasn't abandoned me for He has told me He will never leave me nor forsake me. I am royalty! I'm a child of the King! You spirits of fear, gloom and self-hate must leave. I command you to depart from me in the name of Jesus Christ."

Then start thanking God out loud for every good thing you can think of. Your health, eyesight, strong limbs, salvation, food in the house, etc., etc. Then begin to sing about Jesus. That fear will go! You will have overcome the enemy with the blood of the Lamb and the spoken words of your testimony.

Then too, we have the invitation from Christ concerning *wisdom*. "If any of you lack wisdom, let him ask of God that giveth to all men liberally, and upbraideth not . . ." James, Chapter 1.

What a competitive tool this gives us! How would you like to have free consulting privileges night and day, year after year, from the outstanding experts in all the world?

How much better that *God Himself* has invited us to ask Him for the wisdom we need, and has promised to generously respond. Wow! I have availed myself of this extraordinary privilege in my business. So many times at a point of decision I have sought God and He has always answered. As I look back to those days before I knew Christ, I wonder how, as a businessman, I ever operated without Him. I didn't do as well, either. Twice I have been lauded by associates for coming up with an excellent solution to a problem. I had to explain that this had come from the Lord. It's fascinating to observe in business that the more we pray the smarter we look. Christians know it's not by our might nor power, but by His Spirit.

MOUNTING UP WITH WINGS

The extra energy and relief from weariness that is available to the Christian serving God is still another of His bonus provisions. God has promised, ". . . they that wait upon the Lord shall renew their strength; they shall mount up with wings as eagles; they shall run, and not be weary; and they shall walk, and not faint" Isaiah, Chapter 40.

In recent years I have been awed by the supernatural supply of energy I have had when engaged in Christian work. Especially on the occasion of some speaking itineraries, I have felt this energy flowing in every atom of my being. At times it is necessary to work night and day for long stretches. The kind of schedule that can exhaust body and mind apart from the promise of God. But I have personally discovered that you really can run and not be weary, and walk and not faint when you move in His Spirit. It works! The world would pay much for this flow of divine energy, but it's only for God's own. The devil has only his flawed substitutes—pills and alcohol. They just enslave and sicken.

HOT LINE TO HEAVEN

The Christian has the opportunity to energize his day with prayer. Before work each day I like to thank God for my work and the tools He has provided. For my health and a sound mind. I like to commit the day to Him before picking up the first paper clip.

Then I find value in prayer before each appointment. These preappointment prayers bring results.

And try prayer before *each* decision. How wonderful to see the quality of decisions improve when mixed with prayer.

At the end of the day send up a prayer of thanksgiving. He does so much for us even on our worst days. How good it is to talk and work in partnership with Him. We must not be like the lepers who grieved Christ by forgetting to come back to express thanks. Prayer never slows a day. It's like a supercharger. Making the Holy Spirit a part of every component of your day stretches output. "The effectual fervent prayer of a righteous man availeth much" James, Chapter 5.

LITTLE BLACK LIES

The Christian's mind is more productive because it is free from the burden of lying. We have all met someone who is a persistent liar. Notice that liars never attain much in life. Successful business people have learned that their word must be good. Billions are transacted on the exchange of only a handshake or a verbal signal. Integrity is mandatory. There's no room for a liar in the executive suite. Then too, the liar bears another great disadvantage. His mind is cluttered trying to remember what he said before. The mind of a person who tells the truth isn't fumbling to recall those previous webs of fabrication. Do you see it? The path of success is enhanced by a mind that doesn't have to drag the deadweight of lies. The Christian who will think and work steadfastly will succeed far beyond his fellow workers.

It is an unprecedented hour of opportunity for the Christian. Today firms are earnestly searching for dependable people. The Christian stands out now as his boss compares him with the faltering man of the world. Employers are discovering this last pocket of excellent men and women who are still ready to give them a good day's work. Businesses are increasingly phoning the churches looking for men. With business thefts increasing, and absenteeism from drinking soaring, the Christian looks more and more like a prize. So—don't be bashful about listing your faith on the application next time. Many worldly businessmen now want a godly person on their team. Potiphar felt this way about Joseph. "And his master saw that the Lord was with him, and that the Lord made all that he did to prosper in his hand" Genesis, Chapter 39.

If there is a single key to success and prosperity in the natural realm it is WORK. A quick study of the prosperous shows a pattern of hard and effective work. A study of the failures reveals laziness and undisciplined use of time. We live in a country that still has fabulous opportunities for success. If you want to be a success to honor the name of Christ and to help spread the gospel—talk to the Lord. He wants to help His children excel for His name's sake.

Are you prepared to apply the energy and discipline to succeed? The Bible says: "I wish above all things that thou mayest prosper and be in health . . ." 3 John. God tells us to do whatever we undertake with all our might as unto Him. This requires both prayer and hard work. God puts a premium on those who are willing to be overcomers and press through adversity. Do you have the courage to aim high? God is willing to back you. The road to success is a hard and sometimes lonely one, but He will go with you and before you. It will cut down on your TV, hunting, fishing, golf, sleeping, ball games, and things that please our SELF life. Do you still want to? If your answer is yes, then apply the certain success manual—His Bible. "Keep therefore the words of this covenant, and do them, that ye may prosper in all that ye do" Deuteronomy, Chapter 29.

The personal and financial affairs of a Christian must be orderly for the highest efficiency from his life. He should, for example, be punctual in his appointments, considerate of the time of others, meticulous in the paying of his bills, prompt in correspondence and never a procrastinator.

Sloppiness in these areas and similar life routines bring confusion and cut into prosperity. The successful man is organized and a doer. Our God is not the author of confusion.

The rhythm of life cycles and the precision of the universe bear testimony to the punctuality of God's nature. We should emulate our successful Father in all His ways. "Be ye therefore followers of God . . ." Ephesians, Chapter 5.

The man who puts things off until he feels like doing them soon stumbles over his jumbled pile of unfinished things. His life bogs down with unproductivity and lost opportunities. He never prospers.

The successful man fulfills each obligation immediately, then forgets it, and goes on to the next. Such a man becomes highly effective. He accomplishes a great deal more than the procrastinator.

There is another aid to high productivity. It is one of the secrets many of the successful utilize. Set *hard deadlines* for yourself— a difficult goal. When I follow an ASAP schedule on a project it seems to take forever to get it done. It hangs over me and too many times never gets done.

Most people have thought of things that are truly valuable. They will do them "someday." But "someday" rarely comes. We Christians must seize both time and circumstance and make them work for us. We, through God, have been designed to overcome— to subdue the earth. . . .

My wife kids me about the self-imposed tight scheduling of my life. She says I'm always fighting deadlines. But I know that I am lazy at heart and must discipline myself to work around it.

The Lord has helped me to overcome this lazy flaw by playing constructive games with my time.

When I set a very difficult target to complete something, it's amazing how much extra production I seem to squeeze out. None of us begin to strain our full work potential. This deadline discipline will work for the student, the housewife, and the minister, as well as for the executive. It's for a reason that it is said: "If you need something done, give it to a busy man." He has learned to set deadlines.

You know, it makes life more satisfying too. It's more fun, and it's a prosperity booster to mow through stacks of work.

Enthusiasm is a basic success ingredient. A winner is invariably excited about what he's doing. Just tolerating a job stifles success. Talk to a millionaire and watch him light up when you ask about his work.

The Lord gave us a success formula. He said in effect, "Whatever you undertake, do it with all your might, as unto Me." For a Christian to excel in whatever he is doing exalts the name of Christ. It also brings success. Both the Lord and the world admire an honest winner. We Christians should sparkle with both excitement and productivity. We were born as losers, but reborn to be winners through Christ!

6

GREENER PASTURES

The warp in our nature coupled with a latent optimism often combine to hurtle undisciplined Christians toward financial loss. The same impulse that drives a man with a gambling spirit to sell his tools to buy horserace tickets lurks to trap the Christian in more subtle ways. It can take many forms. . . .

Since I am a businessman, I am visited by Christians caught up in this spirit. Some men seem always to be searching for some get-rich-quick program. They hunt for something to circumvent the disciplined, solid route to prosperity. Sometimes Christians become especially vulnerable when their desires burn to do more for the Lord.

Typically, one will have become genuinely set afire for God and then begin to pray for opportunity to do more for Him. It is in this stage that the unwary can become prey to unwise impulses.

Undisciplined zeal may take various forms. Some become wide open for outlandish financial schemes. They become targets for all kinds of inventors, franchisers, land speculators and even chain letter schemes. Their new desire for financial plenty may, if they aren't careful, cause their hope to overwhelm their wisdom. Some are prone at such a time to borrow large sums of money to put into some venture in a completely unknown field. The fervent Christian seems temporarily blinded by a glow of foolish optimism. The grass always looks greener in those unfamiliar pastures. As he moves in such a state he will then pray for God to prosper his foolish move. The Lord wants us to mix *prayer* and *wisdom* with our zeal. The loser will often blame God when the venture fails.

Another will quit his job abruptly and announce that he is now trusting God for the supply to his family. He forgets Paul who ministered *and* worked. Paul supplied for himself plus enough extra to support other missionary efforts. It is true that God may at times lead one to quit his job and cast himself on the body of Christ for his supply. But far too many make that decision themselves, and then are disappointed in God when things get lean. That isn't God's failure, but the fruit of an unwise human impulse.

Then there are those genuinely zealous for God who will fall into another error. They get to feeling that the end in gaining funds for God justifies almost any means to accomplish it—even un-Scriptural methods. God is consistent throughout His makeup. He abhors many of the ways and means a few Christians use in the raising of funds.

God can only bless truth and honesty, in the raising of money for His works. He doesn't wink at impropriety even for a noble cause. He still calls it sin.

"For I the Lord love judgment, I hate robbery for burnt offering; and I will direct their work in truth . . ." Isaiah, Chapter 61.

When it is improperly done in His name it is almost blasphemous and gives the impression to the world that God is poor and deceitful.

Have you noticed that those Christian endeavors that are spiritually effective and honorable in their fund raising always seem to enjoy adequate finances? Where many are being saved, healed, and where the Spirit of God is moving, there never seems to be a financial crisis. There seems to be no need for strong-arm or pressurized fund raising methods in these ministries.

Human schemes that work on an emotional level are prone to gimmicks. But when men's spirits are really touched through a ministry, their pocketbooks are opened to it.

Fund raising chain letters, dances, lotteries and bingo are obvious examples of odious money schemes for God's work. Odious also to God are exaggerated claims of any Christian work. Inferring full support for orphans or missionaries when it is a partial truth cannot receive God's backing. Using monies given for a specific gospel project, for other things is abhorrent to God. Embellishing testimonies or reports of the numbers saved are disappointing to Him. His work needs no embroidery.

God doesn't think "evangelistically speaking" is funny. It is dishonest in His eyes and He cannot bless. No wonder some works are desperate. It isn't always the devil that is holding back their money.

On the other hand, it is imperative that we lay Christians be forthrightly taught by men of God how to give. One of the most difficult jobs for a pastor, teacher or evangelist lies in this very realm. We should be most sensitive and responsive to a ministry's needs. Paul wasn't bashful about sharp exhortation in this vital Christian area.

Some otherwise courageous pastors feel browbeaten and apologetic when taking an offering. It is his privilege and his duty to train us concerning the blessings of God inherent in Scriptural giving. Let's encourage them and be more responsive in this basic Christian privilege.

7

TRUE CONFESSIONS

One day after Judson had suffered a long series of failures in his dream to bring the gospel to India, his board timidly wrote to him. They asked how under the circumstances he still viewed his prospects in India. His return letter said, "My prospects are still as bright as the promises of God." Until that time he had not seen one convert. From that very moment on he commenced to see tens of thousands accept Christ throughout India.

Certain cults are operating on the very edge of a great truth involving positive confession in the money area. A number of these large groups that are otherwise off-center preach prosperity and health. Some refuse even to acknowledge or speak the words *poverty* and *illness*. They treat them as an illusion. This teaching, although unbalanced, brings certain positive results in their lives and we can learn something from them.

Their absence of negative confession is helpful, and you see an unusual percentage of the prosperous sitting in their pews. Mind over matter and self-confidence are short of God's Word. His best is unbending confidence in the Word in every circumstance. Judson's positive confession of God's promises exploded into the prosperity of his India work.

Words are creative! We have no idea how powerful they really are, for good or for ill. (See James, Chapter 3.) God *spoke* the world into being. The very expression of God—Jesus Christ—isn't called the Word for nothing. Jesus said we could in faith move a huge mountain, with a positive faith-drenched confession.

The communists know the power of oral confession. They developed brainwashing and they teach their young to repeat in groups the thoughts of Marx, Lenin and Mao. Speaking oaths is a powerful technique of even the most evil works. The Mau Mau, the witch doctor, the Mafia and secret societies know the force of oaths. The Black Mass's confession of Satan's power brings down demonic activity.

Even the nonbelieving athlete knows the power of confession. Mohammed Ali isn't clowning when before a fight he beats his breast and cries, "I am the greatest!" A college team and its cheering section will roar, "We're number one!" And it helps!

Motivation experts teach a star salesman to look boldly in his mirror each morning and say, "Today nothing can stop me. I'm going to have the greatest sales ever"

The zenith of human attainment isn't gotten with a man's brains or his fists. That zenith—the ultimate for man—is eternal life beside the Lord of the universe! This is attainable through his lips. ". . . confess with thy mouth the Lord Jesus, and . . . thou shalt be saved . . . with the mouth confession is made unto salvation" Romans, Chapter 10.

Prayer is more powerful than hydrogen bombs. Dr. Alexis Carrel, a Nobel prizewinner said, "Prayer is the strongest form of generative energy."

A word to the Lord brings down wonderful supernatural happenings. Salvation, healing, financial help, peace of mind, protection, miracles, etc. All these through asking in harmony with God's written Word. Positive confession creates positive happenings! But many Christians confess negatively and these can prolong unfortunate circumstances. The Christian hypochondriac will for example remain in a continuous state of sickness and cannot be healed as long as she spews from her mouth testimony of her illnesses. She is actually exalting the victories of sickness and Satan over her. This is no climate for Christ the Healer to work in.

God has given that woman the free will to keep her sicknesses if she wants them. Her sickness, not Christ, is the subject of her conversation. Some even use their sicknesses to cop out on life responsibilities. Others milk an inferior kind of love from their woes. We call it sympathy. Yes, they can retain constant sicknesses by their confessions, just as the faithful Christian can trigger healing by confessing Christ's promises.

Don't just sympathize alone for someone needing a victory. Fleshly sympathy can at times create a climate that thwarts spiritual triumph. Those in need would benefit more by the spending of our *faith* than just the spending of our sympathy in their behalf.

We have all felt at some time the gloomy forces created by negative confession. Someone will come up and forlornly say, "Poor you. You look so tired," or, "You poor thing. You just don't look well today."

Suddenly your spirits sag! That is, unless you take authority over it with a bright, "Thanks, but praise God, I'm fine!"

Smith Wigglesworth had to kick two sympathizing, fear-infected parents right out of a sick child's room before he could successfully speak the prayer of victory over their dying girl.

Jesus had to drive sympathizing, scoffing friends from a house before even He could speak the words of life over one who was dead. These same victory principles work in every realm of our life. Health, finances, marriage, business, ministry, etc., etc. Then, too, because of God's promises we should be expecting victories, not defeats. Be expecting blessings, not trouble! Be like the faith-charged prophet who prayed for rain and confidently looked for the cloud. It poured.

I want to share a mundane little secret. If I have experienced this once, it has been thirty times. Whenever I would sneeze and start to feel punk in the days before I was a Christian, I would promptly confess it to the handiest person, "Oh, oh, I've caught a cold." I promptly welcomed that cold, never imagining there was an alternative.

When this happens now, I immediately say out loud something like this, "I don't have time for a cold. You have no place in me, you foul disease, and I will have no part of you. By Jesus' stripes I am healed and by His blood I am cleansed and I won't receive you. I cast you from me in the name of Jesus Christ, this instant!"

You know, I am continually delighted how this simple kind of prayer works. It seems most effective when confessed as the first symptom of trouble appears, and sometimes before you can prove that you have a problem. It will work for you in every type of problem that looms up. God's promises and provisions are for our use against every problem, and in every crisis. ". . . whatsoever ye shall ask in prayer, believing, ye shall receive." Matthew, Chapter 22. (See also John, Chapter 3 and John, Chapter 16.)

GOD LOVES A WINNER

God wants us to learn to wield His victory weapons in all life circumstances. Some people will allow poverty and defeat to harass them all through life. They will say, "I guess the Lord just meant us to be poor and to suffer these many years of trials. Pray that we'll be able to endure them."

You know of such Christians who seem to live in a constant chain of trouble and crises. Often they are the ones who will testify of them at every opportunity and who live in expectancy of more. The Oh-my-I-wonder-what's-next syndrome.

God receives no joy whatsoever in seeing His children downtrodden, financially strapped and overrun with defeats. (See 1 Corinthians 10.) Our Father isn't a sadist. Sure, He allows trials to test and develop our faith for a reason, but that's all. Yes, after Eden all men were born as losers, but God provided that each could be reborn as a winner.

God fashions no trophies for the ones constantly overrun by Satan in this world. He has no pleasure seeing them constantly downtrodden by the enemy. You say, "That sounds harsh."

Well, the Lord gave us all power over the enemy. He wants us to use these victory weapons He forged at Calvary for such a time. Weapons are for use, not for conversation pieces. He doesn't enjoy sad, beaten-down children, as much as those happy, obedient ones who learned to win using His provisions. God loves winners! Did you know that?

Beloved, listen to His heart concerning winners. He loves those that overcome by the blood of the Lamb and by the word of their testimony. His heavenly prizes aren't for those Christians who insist on living behind Satan's eight ball because of their neglect of His victory provisions. These trophies are for His winners.

"To him that overcometh will I give to eat of the tree of life, which is in the midst of the paradise of God" Revelation, Chapter 2.

"To him that overcometh will I give to eat of the hidden manna, and will give him a white stone, and in the stone a new name written" Chapter 2.

"He that overcometh, and keepeth my works unto the end, to him will I give power over the nations: And he shall rule them with a rod of iron; as the vessels of a potter shall they be broken to shivers: even as I received of my Father. And I will give him the morning star" Chapter 2.

"He that overcometh, the same shall be clothed in white raiment; and I will not blot out his name out of the book of life, but I will confess his name before my Father, and before his angels" Chapter 3.

"Him that overcometh will I make a pillar in the temple of my God, and he shall go no more out: and I will write upon him the name of my God, and the name of the city of my God . . ." Chapter 3.

"To him that overcometh will I grant to sit with me in my throne, even as I also overcame, and am set down with my Father in his throne" Chapter 3.

Now let's begin to operate in the financial realm and our general life in *this* Spirit. Don't be one to whom the Lord can say ". . . Ye have not, because ye ask not" James, Chapter 4. Don't be satisfied either with just a little improvement in your life's affairs after your prayer of faith.

When we have a big problem and pray for a solution we sometimes pinch off the Spirit's flow toward a total victory by our satisfaction with just the relief from the crisis phase.

When you ask our mighty God for victory don't be satisfied with a partial answer. He wants our faith and our expectancy to see the matter all the way through to a God-size victory. He wants us to learn to live on Overcoming Street in all departments of Christian life and ministry.

Harald Bredesen says, "God's heart is more grieved by the satisfiedness of the saints than by the wickedness of the sinners."

"A man shall be satisfied with good by the fruit of his mouth . . ." Proverbs, Chapter 12.

Yes, God loves for His children to become winners through His provision!

8

JOB'S SECRET

Roger Anderson was the best teacher First Baptist ever had, and Marion, his wife, was the choir director. Both of their sons were in seminary at Wheaton.

Roger was a football star at O.S.U. and after graduation he entered the export-import business. After fourteen years he had become an established expert in foreign trade. Not only had he become a millionaire, but he had become so able that he was sought for counsel on occasion by the Commerce Department.

Roger felt a definite call on his life for the ministry as a teenager during a summer camp meeting. This receded in his mind as athletic popularity struck, but the call still arose periodically. It flared up just a few months after he met Marion. During one summer they both talked about the day they could leave together for the mission field. After they were married they put it off to accumulate more funds. Then success rose to smother the call. They rationalized their staying home by extra giving to mission projects and by their Sunday work at the church. In his case God wasn't looking for Roger's money, but for Roger. There was a disobedience lurking behind this churchman, even though he was their church's outstanding layman.

There came an hour when his loving and patient God began to move in his behalf. Roger was now prosperous, but increasingly unsuccessful in life. Even with all these things going for him, there was a nagging unhappiness. His affluence hadn't brought inner joy. Roger finally let his business pull him from serving God and then things started to come unglued. . . . ". . . As long as he sought the Lord, God made him to prosper" Chronicles, Chapter 26.

His international business began to get more hazardous. Roger's largest accounts were in Chile, Argentina and Japan. The Argentina currency dropped sharply. A large account in Chile was expropriated, and the upward adjustments in the exchange rate for the Japanese yen suddenly ruined his supplier in Osaka.

Roger's bank honored a giant letter of credit for a shipment of chemicals that could only be sold at a loss. Now his friendly banker was on the phone for more collateral. He asked for more than Roger had. This had all piled up in eleven months and it was grim!

In the midst of this a chest soreness of Marion's proved malignant and Roger himself was laid up with mononucleosis two months later.

A household that eleven months earlier seemed set for life was now struggling with both a Chapter XI bankruptcy and one catastrophic sickness.

Friends rallied to them but they also became a topic of debate. Some of it went like this: "The Andersons seemed to be such good people. How could God do such things?" "There must be some darkness in their lives." "God seems to have turned His back on the Andersons." "God must be bringing judgment on them for something. I wonder if Roger is honest in that business?" On and on. . . .

Marion's faith seemed shattered by the multiple blows, but somehow Roger's seemed to rise. People couldn't understand his attitude. "Wasn't he remorseful about his creditors?" "Didn't he care about Marion?" They forgot that the Bible says: "For whom the Lord loveth he chasteneth" Hebrews, Chapter 6.

After the first few setbacks Roger started to blame God and rolled up his sleeves to work out his own solution. But deep inside him was the good seed God had planted in his youth. The seed blossomed in the crisis to choke out the tares of fear.

He began to pray as he hadn't done since those camp nights. He began to see how far he had drifted from God. Roger said, "Why, I never knew I was just playing church. I just slipped into a *form* of godliness."

Roger cried out for mercy and asked forgiveness for blaming God. He remembered how he had failed to thank Him in all those years of plenty, and now sensed that he had inwardly taken the credit for all his success. He sought forgiveness for the disobedience toward God's call. Roger began to notice things in his Bible that he had never considered relevant before. He rediscovered God's Treasure Map.

Scriptures on healing brought new hope. The Andersons had developed confidence in Dr. Kilpatrick. He was the best and had never failed them—BEFORE. But Marion was getting beyond even the expertise of Dr. Kilpatrick or even his specialist friends in Rochester. God's blessings come in more forms than just cash. He often thunders in riches that cash cannot buy.

Roger and Marion in their desperation finally turned all the way to God. Jehova-Rapha with His infinite love and healing virtue touched first Roger and then Marion, both within four months. They were ecstatic, and began to testify of their double miracle and wrote a magazine article about it.

Several months later in the new atmosphere of faith the Anderson's business affairs began to show faint signs of life. While Roger was struck down, his number-three man had somehow just taken charge, and had ably struggled with the violent forces that tore at the business.

Roger thought that only he could run the business and had never learned to delegate responsibility. He had shown little confidence in the judgment of his executive staff on large decisions. Stan, his accounting chief, was accordingly untried. No one ever knew of Stan's hidden reservoir of strength until the crisis.

Stan somehow began finding assets in some of Roger's dormant accounts and turned large losses in others to moderate ones. Fourteen months after those first crippling blows struck, Roger's phone rang. It was his banker. "Roger, I want to compliment you on the almost miraculous job that you and Stan have done with the company. This morning you were released by the referee from all vestiges of the bankruptcy proceedings, and further, your accounts are current at last. The bank will be pleased to work with you now and in the future. You really proved your 'metal' in this furnace."

Roger was caught off guard, but he had started praying even as his banker poured out the good news. A leading from God grew in Roger's throat and startled him as it did. He was at a crossroad. God was giving him another chance. . . .

As the banker finished speaking, Roger began, haltingly. He

awkwardly told how *God* had saved his business. It grew easier as he went along and he told of Marion's healing and his own rediscovery of the Lord. Roger sensed a remarkable openness in his banker and decided to forge ahead. For the first time in his life he led a man to Christ by telephone.

The telephone conversation with the banker just clinched something in Roger's heart! He looked back and marveled at God's patience with him. How the Lord had prospered him even while he walked in disobedience to that call to the ministry. He could now understand why the financial prosperity had still left him empty. His soul had grown leaner as he drifted both from his call and from the Lord.

The multiple troubles that had rained on the Anderson household had drawn him back to God. Without them Roger now realized he would have continued to live below his spiritual potential. Neither Marion nor he would have discovered God's deeper benefits. An overwhelming gratitude came to him for the Lord's mercy. *Trouble* had served Roger as a friend.

Those troubles he had so resisted and complained about had proved to be the perfect medicine for his life! He covenanted with God right there to entrust the Anderson Company to Stan's direction and turn to full-time Christian work. When he did so, he said a peace flowed over him like warm honey.

Some ministers inadvertently overstress superficial blessings in life. They speak so positively of never ending victories. "Something good is going to happen." There's a twist among certain otherwise great evangelists and ministers that makes it sound almost like mind over matter. The Bible also says: ". . . all things work together for good to them that love God . . ." Romans, Chapter 8. In Roger's case "all things" looked at first like bankruptcy and sickness.

Overstressing serenity and not balancing it with the other important side can leave Christians bewildered. When one goes out of such meetings and encounters the reality of life's buffetings he may erroneously feel he is a hopeless case, an inferior Christian. Why can't he live in this constant state of victory over everything and have constant prosperity? Well, he has inadvertently received only half of the complete lesson. That evangelist doesn't live in perpetual pink bliss either. He, too, is still learning how to better apply God's Word in the streets of life. There are still problems every week in the life of even the most mature Christian.

Remember that any learning process includes both success and failure. Don't ever become discouraged with your own life when you hear a stream of victorious testimonies. Those of us who share these true and magnificent victory reports could also share equally true stories of our dramatic failures.

Then there is that Job effect. A most depressing chain of calamities came to Job. They looked for all the world like God's judgments. Just as Job's friends tried to read something into his problems, Roger Anderson's did the same.

Although we should be expectant for victories and learn to be overcomers, certain problems can be useful. To develop his muscles the weight lifter must press against heavy iron. To develop our faith "muscles" God allows His children to press from time to time against problems and adversities. These can serve not only to test our faith, but to make it strong.

Yes, trouble can be a servant. Don't always run from it, for it may have been sent for our good, by a wise and loving Father. Job passed his tests. He said, "Though he slay me, yet will I trust in him . . ." Job, Chapter 13.

When he did, God not only began to graduate Job from his "trouble class," but doubled his prosperity.

Roger Anderson is today a bright servant in God's full-time army. He and Marion know a richness in life they were never able to find in their millions. The hero in the Andersons' life wasn't *trouble,* but their rediscovery of the practical riches in *God's Word.* Victory is in Christ's Word—trouble can be used to prove it!

9

LITTLE SHAFTS OF LIGHT

The word *polarization* has I suppose always been in the dictionary, but never has it enjoyed the usage it does today.

This term is used in the study of many of the sciences, such as geology, mathematics, and physics. But it is in sociology that we now hear it so much. Polarization of east versus west. Of the right versus left. Polarization of the races. Of the haves versus the have-nots, etc.

The list is extensive. Society is fragmenting at a swift rate. However, in no area is polarizing more evident than in the realm of the two classes of society which we label the Establishment and the *anti*-Establishment. Their controversy includes the subject of *material possessions*.

The *anti* group charges the members of the Establishment with greed, materialism, hypocrisy and amorality.

On the other hand those of the Establishment call the *antis* lazy, irresponsible, parasitic and immoral.

Let's look at a few of the things that God has to say on materialism, possessions, gain, and money. In the final analysis it's God who always has the last word.

In the Old Testament, righteousness and prosperity in this world seemed almost synonymous. This viewpoint was carried over in the thinking of the people right up to Jesus' time.

Jesus spoke thirty-five parables that are recorded in the gospels. Of these, more than a third deal directly or indirectly with the subject of money and material possessions. Jesus came into the world and quietly began to speak as no man ever spoke before. His parables are profound. At first they seem childlike and simple. Further study reveals their mystery and deep running wisdom. Jesus' parables seem as foolish enigmas to the wordly genius, however they are pools of light and truth to the simplest believer.

Dr. Follette once challenged an intellectual who was scoffing at the simple-sounding parables of Jesus. Follette challenged him to write just one simple parable, truth-filled and understandable for the simple believer, yet incomprehensible to the unbeliever with a high I.Q. He failed!

As Christ spoke with authority on the subjects of sin and righteousness and judgment, He opened up a whole new life concept. Jesus *illumined* and *fulfilled* the law that God's earlier prophets had written. Christ's words—on any given subject—reveal for us the mind of the Father:

". . . but he that sent me is true; and I speak to the world those things which I have heard of him" John, Chapter 8.

". . . I do nothing of myself; but as my Father hath taught me, I speak these things" Chapter 8.

"For I have not spoken of myself; but the Father which sent me . . ." Chapter 12.

Thus Christ spoke for the Father who controls the universe. His words are pregnant with the secrets of life and prosperity.

There is a beautiful balance in all that Jesus taught in regard to financial matters and it bears the unchanging principles for today's Christian.

CAESAR'S BUREAU OF INTERNAL REVENUE

"Then went the Pharisees, and took counsel how they might entangle him in his talk . . ." Matthew, Chapter 22.

Then came the clever question which they thought He could not answer without completely entangling Himself: "Tell us therefore, what thinkest thou? Is it lawful to give tribute unto Caesar, or not" Chapter 22?

But these men didn't have a chance for they were dealing with the One who knows all inner motives. He wasn't intimidated by the questioning of foolish men. They soon discovered how true were their own words, ". . . for thou regardest not the person of men" Chapter 22. For Jesus perceived their wickedness and called them hypocrites. He knew that the thing closest to their hearts was their pocketbook and not the desire for truth. Jesus called for someone to show Him a coin. Upon being questioned, they agreed that the image and superscription thereon was that of "President" Caesar.

Then came Christ's Word which transcended their expectation. "Render therefore unto Caesar the things which are Caesar's; and unto God the things that are God's" Chapter 22. He threw a bright light on the two distinct realms and taught the honoring of the rights of each of these realms.

A perfect balance! An answer that settles similar questions in our time as well. It's no wonder "they marvelled . . . and went their way" Chapter 22.

Let us, accordingly, never grieve the Lord in our own life by failing to render unto Caesar all that is Caesar's. This is as displeasing to the Lord as failing to render unto God the things that are of His realm.

Caesar's realm of authority includes not only taxes, but all governmental matters, and God tells us to pray for all men and those in authority. Let us be obedient to our leaders and to our government and all its laws *as unto God*. The Bible tells us that secular authority is given by God and we are to obey and honor it, too, in its proper realm in society. (See Romans, Chapter 13.) Never be found undermining, mocking, cheating, or resisting those in authority. We can deal with them in the voting booth.

Even Christ rendered to Caesar's bureau of taxation. It was so galling to the Israelites to have a temple tax levied on them; but Jesus didn't blow on their smoldering feelings of resentment. He led no riots. He kept Caesar's laws. He said, "Notwithstanding, lest we should offend them. . . ." and provided for Himself and also for Peter the money to meet the secular law's demands.

"And when they were come to Capernaum, they that received tribute money came to Peter, and said, Doth not your master pay tribute? He saith, Yes. And when he was come into the house, Jesus prevented him, saying, What thinkest thou, Simon? of whom do the kings of the earth take custom or tribute? of their own children or of strangers? Peter saith unto him, Of strangers. Jesus saith unto him, Then are the children free. Notwithstanding, lest we should offend them, go thou to the sea, and cast an hook, and take up the fish that first cometh up; and when thou hast opened his mouth, thou shalt find a piece of money: that take, and give unto them for me and thee" Matthew, Chapter 17.

Some have scoffed at Peter for having said ". . . Lord, we have left all, and followed thee" Luke, Chapter 18. Such people say that Peter had been only a fisherman and had nothing to leave.

But let's face it. Peter was a businessman, with a boat, nets and family. At the call of Jesus he left his business and trudged up and down the land of Judea, following and serving the Son of God who had won his heart. Month followed month and year followed year because Jesus had said, "Come . . . and I will make you to become fishers of men" Mark, Chapter 1. Peter loved and trusted the Lord more than his Peter Fishing Company.

How many of us can say, "Lord, we have left all to follow you"? If we can answer, Yes, then we too qualify for His promise, "But my God shall supply all your need according to His riches in glory by Christ Jesus" Philippians, Chapter 4. Our Lord will intervene for our needs just as He did for Peter's taxes and daily bread when we too seek first the Kingdom of God and His righteousness. Thousands have tested Him on this promise and have found Him more than sufficient.

It's thrilling to see how again in our day thousands of businessmen follow that same Jesus with fervor and integrity. He is still providing for them too.

10

DIAL H-E-A-V-E-N

Praying for one another in times of crisis is the Scripture's formula, and it still works in today's chrome and glass business settings. That early church called on God in time of need. The Bible says we are to bear one another's burdens. It also tells us that the prayers of a righteous man availeth much.

The prayer-chain telephone rang a few months ago to signal Carl's king-sized business crisis. He is a deacon at Valley Church and manager of Carl's Trucking Company. For years he has supplied jobs for dozens of Christians and good hauling service for one of the largest toy manufacturers in the country.

Three hours earlier a tough decisive tax agent had walked into the office of Carl's Trucking waving a legal paper. He demanded twenty thousand dollars immediately to satisfy a disputed tax claim. After ten minutes of accusations and abuse in front of Carl's stunned employees, he shut the company down.

The employees were filtering out of the building when the phone rang. As Carl reached for the phone the agent caught his wrist, "Those phones don't belong to you anymore. Carl's Trucking is finished!"

Carl's home and his car had been mortgaged the year before to increase operating capital for his growing business. He had no personal reserves and had reached his borrowing limit at the bank to repair their earthquake-damaged house. It was hopeless! He called home and then called the church.

Two hours after that prayer-chain phone call there were six men praying in Carl's living room. The prayers took on a pattern under the Holy Spirit's guidance. First, there were specific prayers for a change in the heart of that tax agent. Second, there were prayers for the twenty thousand, and enough more to put Carl's Trucking on a permanently solid operating level. We told the Lord that a "patch" to tide over Carl's crisis wasn't enough. We asked Him for a total healing of the business.

The following morning at eleven o'clock Carl received an unsolicited call from the agent volunteering seven more days to secure the twenty thousand. In less than a week, not one but two individuals came to Carl to work out ways to invest substantial new funds in his trucking firm. Yes, God answers His phone when His children call!

The Lord says woe to the one that hasn't another to lift him up when he falls.

A similar case may further illustrate this great plan of God's to honor prayers of His children for one another.

One day Harald Bredesen, Paul Lincoln and I drove to Pasadena to meet Steve Lazarian and his wife. When we arrived they were standing outside the office of their handsome building. The place seemed large for the few people working in it.

While we waited to leave for lunch they were sharing—it was good to hear how the Lazarian Engineering and Construction business was dedicated to God. They told us with delight how this building was being used for weekend Bible studies.

"Our business has prospered for years, but right now we are in a tight place," they said. "We have a crisis!" Over recent months they had spent money to prepare and submit many bids on construction jobs all around Southern California. Every customer had a different reason, and none of their bids had materialized into a job.

The stories had a pattern. One customer would say in effect, "We have your bid, and it's good. We are ready to go ahead on our new building, but the bank doesn't have the money for new construction right now, so we can't go ahead with the job." One after another of these expensive proposals had melted into nothingness! "Look around," they said, "and see all the empty drafting tables—but our Lord is good and He will somehow bring us through this. Please remember us in your prayers."

Now it was time for lunch, and we were all walking along together between their building and the parking lot, moving along in a loose, strung out group. It wasn't until right then that I responded to a persistent thought—one of those strong impulses!

After another twenty-five or thirty steps I called out to those ahead, "Say, could we just take a moment for prayer, even before we go to lunch? Could we all go back inside for a minute? I feel we are to pray right now for Steve's business."

We all turned around and filed back into the building. As Steve opened the door to one of the rooms he said, "We can pray in here—it's not too hard to find an empty office right now." We stood silently for a few moments holding hands, and then started to pray.

Dear Lord, we cry out to You, in behalf of Steve's company. We bind you, Satan, from any further interference in the bids and finances of this business! It is written that what we bind on earth in the name of Jesus, shall be bound in heaven, and we now bind every spirit and every circumstance coming against Steve's business and in Jesus' name right now we loose those contracts! We thank You, Lord, that You said if two of us shall agree concerning *anything* in Your name that it SHALL be done. We now agree together for victory here. Thank You for hearing and answering our prayers.

We had only taken a couple of minutes from our luncheon schedule. Two weeks later, Harald Bredesen phoned. "Have you heard about Lazarian's business?" I said, "No, I haven't. Are there any new developments yet?"

Harald said, "Steve's employees are telling an 'in' joke over there. Their business is flooding in right now, and they are kiddingly asking Steve to get hold of that fellow over in Northridge and ask him to stop praying."

Yes, it's going to be vital in these hard days to pray for one another—imperative to remember our "throne rights" as believers. If we are hit with financial calamity the remedy is in His Word. When struck with natural obstacles and distress, be quick to seek supernatural recourse. Great walls are for the leaping—through Christ! "For by thee I have run through a troop; and by my God have I leaped over a wall" Psalms, Chapter 18.

Remember, all power in heaven and earth was given to Christ and He has delegated that power to us—the believers. Use it!

11

VIOLATION OF THE LAMBS

Senator Birch Bayh recently said that research has shown that more than a million teen-agers are now running away each year. They found that this runaway rate has drastically increased in the last four years. We are experiencing a catastrophic weakening of our national vitality in the dropouts among our new generation.

Parents are charged by God with the life preparation responsibility for their young. "Train up a child in the way he should go . . ." Proverbs, Chapter 22, He said, and we are failing Him. Even the animals obey Him.

The communist countries know the power of shaping the young mind. They take over the very young and mold their minds into near robot attitudes and behaviors. America waxed strong as the pioneer parents developed godliness in their children. Early on-the-job training developed a nation of Yankees that catapulted America to world leadership, and the young were taught more than craftsmanship.

They grew up respecting the Bible, hard work, thrift, moral values, their country, responsibility and courage. The nation prospered in spirit and substance as those early parents molded their young in harmony with God's Word.

But as the new nation rocketed in strength and wealth, parents grew lax in child-training and discipline. A drift from God accelerated a deterioration in character. The nation had such resources and strength built up that it was able to grow careless and still move ahead for a season through sheer inertia. But a sickness began to show in its face: "For they have sown the wind, and they shall reap the whirlwind . . ." Hosea, Chapter 8.

Our generation has been staggered by the ugly explosion of rebellious youth. The beatnick, the grisly Manson commune, the flower children, the gangs, the child prostitutes, the hippie and the militant student revolutionary! The whirlwind indeed!

But why? They grew up under a corrosive Dr. Spock permissiveness. They were spawned in homes where cold, loveless materialism chilled. Children rushed from school to lonely empty houses. Mother was working to pay for chrome luxuries. Many grew up watching their parents ignoring God, drinking, shading the truth, loving pleasure. Even the birds don't foul their nests!

Most were handed allowance money instead of love and lessons on life's values. Food, presents, clothes, public schooling, cars, movies and money flowed effortlessly with no sense of their relationship to work and productivity. The value of money became distorted. Church and Bible study evaporated from the life-style. Chores, work duties, integrities and responsibilities were absent from youth's preparation to meet life.

Social action, calculus, dissent, Latin, freethinking, sex education, modern art, political science and avant-garde literature in schools hardly equip youth to assume moral charge of their world. Failure to produce a new generation of responsible humans lies first with our generation of parents and second with some of our educators.

When America fell out of love with God to have an affair with education she steered for the rocks. No wonder we see that nomadic army of long-haired, unproductive, ragged, lewd-living, diseased, revolutionary, unhappy, pot-smoking, glassy-eyed, old children.

But *they belong to us!* They are the product of our spiritual folly and the heart of every believer now breaks for them.

Somehow their plight has struck the heart of God. He is now moving among them and miraculously rescuing them in wholesale lots from their pits of despair—we call it the Jesus Movement. It's real and it's big! God is doing in His mercy what we failed to do. He is rescuing among this lost generation. But we will still have to face our God for this colossal sin.

We must shape up as parents. We must get into that Bible ourselves. We must now train up our little children with some dynamic authority and discipline. Teach them to love God and to respect work, integrity and morals. Let's learn to speak that word *No* again. Give them praise and affection when they do right and a rod when they don't. Teach them to prosper in life on this exquisite globe as unto our magnificent God. And let's stop farming out our young for the ungodly to shape. Teach again spiritual and moral values in the home that the nation might live.

Hardest of all—let's start living consistent and godly lives before them!

12

THE FOUNTAINHEAD

In Jesus' day few were despised by the Jews more than one of their own who took the political job of tax collector. He had not only stooped to take employment from the hated Roman government, but was usually a Jew who operated on the principle: If you can't lick them join them. His countrymen knew the tax collector not only gathered the Roman taxes, but wasn't above tacking on extra and pocketing it for himself. Such a fellow was called by profession a *publican,* and he was classed in the minds of the Jews with the sinners, harlots, and heathens.

In Jericho there was such a man. Zacchaeus had three strikes against him with his contemporaries: (1) he was small; (2) he was the top publican; and (3) he was well-to-do.

One hot desert day Jesus Himself walked through the lush oasis town of Jericho. A crowd was thronging Him as usual. This Zacchaeus ". . . sought to see Jesus who he was" Luke, Chapter 19. Because he was short he couldn't even get a glimpse of this One of whom he had heard many stirring reports. Suddenly he spied a sycamore tree.

"And when Jesus came to the place, he looked up, and saw him, and said unto him, Zacchaeus, make haste, and come down; for to day I must abide at thy house" Chapter 19. And he made haste and came down and received Him joyfully. Through one divine contact Zacchaeus was moved upon by the Spirit of God.

But not everyone was pleased! For when they saw it ". . . they all murmured, saying that He was gone to be guest with a man that is a sinner" Chapter 19. But wasn't it the sinners Jesus said He came for? Many of us are long on condemnation and a little short on compassion—especially when *money* is somehow involved.

After seeing Jesus, Zacchaeus was through holding out on God. He carried on no dialogue with others, but instead spoke directly to this Jesus, "Behold, Lord, the half of my goods I give to the poor . . ." Chapter 19. It's doubtful that any in that grumbling throng had ever done as much. How many of us have? He had been born again in his pocketbook, too, for Zacchaeus continued, ". . . and if I have taken anything from any man by false accusation, I restore him fourfold" Chapter 19.

Notice that Jesus hadn't accused Zacchaeus of dishonesty. He came not to condemn but to reconcile. He never reminded Zacchaeus of the laws concerning restitution. He didn't make an offering speech or even pass a plate. But when Zacchaeus got right with Jesus the Holy Spirit did all this in less time than it takes us to read it.

The Holy Spirit is doing the same thing today when people really get to know Jesus. The present-day outpouring of God's Spirit is loosing more purse strings and checkbooks than all of our money crusades combined.

When any person truly encounters Jesus it results in an opened purse. This is beginning to meet the needs of God's work in the world. A revelation of the living Christ is the *fountainhead* of Christian stewardship.

THE GLITTERING IDOL

We are reminded of another man Jesus encountered. We were never told his name. He has only been called the rich young ruler. There are so many about us today. He may live down the block or even in your house.

"And when he was gone forth into the way, there came one running, and kneeled to him, and asked Him, Good Master, what shall I do that I may inherit eternal life? And Jesus said unto him, Why callest thou me good? there is none good but one, that is, God. Thou knowest the commandments, Do not commit adultery, Do not kill, Do not steal, Do not bear false witness, Defraud not, Honour thy father and mother. And he answered and said until him, Master, all these have I observed from my youth. Then Jesus beholding him loved him, and said unto him, One thing thou lackest: go thy way, sell whatsoever thou hast, and give to the poor, and thou shalt have treasure in heaven: and come, take up the cross, and follow me. And he was sad

at that saying, and he went away grieved: for he had great possessions" Mark, Chapter 10. (See also Matthew, Chapter 19,
Luke, Chapter 18.)

This young man who had everything came to Jesus with a
tormenting question. Three of the gospel writers underscore the
importance of this true story. Never get the notion that just because certain people seem to have everything that they don't have
questions or problems concerning life. They may appear unap-
proachable but they're not. God is now doing a great work among
the rich young rulers of our time. There are nearly 300,000 businessmen attending weekly meetings of Christian businessmen's
groups!

Some today who are wealthy but poor in spirit commit suicide;
others live out warped unfulfilled existences. Most rationalize
their emptiness and try to wallpaper it over with jet-setting, work,
society, liquor, parties or even human charities. Not so those
who live the life of High Adventure with God!

I was recently a houseguest of a lovely seventy-year-old widow.
Her husband had founded one of the largest firms in America.
Her net worth exceeds one hundred million. For decades she has
attended a church that has a totally social thrust.

She still labors twelve hours a day receiving people and proposi-
tions for charitable grants. The fruit of her massive holdings is
being dispensed to universities, patriotic endeavors and general
charity.

After prayer and observation God laid a hard burden on my
heart. It became my lot to break the news to her that both her
life and her giving were a disappointment to God. She was shocked
and incredulous at my words!

This dear lady had developed a shiny steel shell around herself
that had kept God away. She had never imagined that she wasn't
among the most pleasing humans in His eyes. Wasn't she working herself to exhaustion in these noble charities?

But she was in truth trying to play God herself. She was giving
her millions in her own name and enjoying the lofty role, secretly
relishing the stream of people with hands extended. She had cast
a shadow on God, who wants to be our supply. She was uninten-
tionally working against God, not in harmony with Him at all.

Her soul had been sickened with acute self-righteousness. You can imagine her reaction when I reminded her that God says such righteousness is, to Him, as filthy rags.

It was necessary to point out as gently as possible that she was actually selfish! God doesn't need her help or her money. It is He who owns not only the cattle on the thousand hills, but the hills themselves from whence her wealth was dug.

She was giving of her millions, but withholding that which God really wanted—herself! Her busyness had shut out the voice of God, and she had never given time to His written Word. The Bible generously gives its directions to avoid all such pitfalls. It finally struck her that she really was a sinner like everyone else and that God sought only her love. Her heart began to melt for Jesus.

Back now to our other rich ruler. His question was simple and direct, and it revealed his void. "What lack I yet?" Matthew, Chapter 19. The answer he received wasn't what he expected. He was looking for approval and assurance but, "Jesus said unto him, If thou wilt be perfect, go and sell that thou hast, and give to the poor, and thou shalt have treasure in heaven: and come follow me. But when the young man heard that saying, he went away sorrowful: for he had great possessions" Chapter 19.

It was a hard saying for the rich man.

When we direct questions to our Greater-than-Solomon, we still receive sure answers—maybe not always what we wanted to hear, but the perfect answers for every problem.

Don't infer from this Scripture that Jesus was directing everyone to sell all that they have and give to the poor. But Jesus looked into that *particular man's* heart and prescribed the essential course for him. Jesus saw that the spirit of the rich young ruler was overwhelmed by his glittering idol—wealth. Jesus wanted him to trust in His Word instead of wealth. If he had been obedient to Christ, he wouldn't ever have lost as a result of his obedience.

In the account of the night visit to Jesus by wealthy Nicodemus, a ruler of the Jews, we see that he too was laden with another heavy question concerning life. Jesus told Nicodemus plainly, "Except a man be born again, he cannot see the kingdom of God" John, Chapter 3, and again, "Except a man be born of water and of the Spirit, he cannot enter into the kingdom of God" Chapter 3, clearly indicating that every man must be born again.

As Weymouth's translation puts it, " 'In very truth I tell you . . . that unless a man is born anew he cannot see the kingdom of God' " Chapter 3.

However, in the encounter with the rich young ruler Jesus made it a *personal* thing by saying, "If thou wilt be perfect . . ." Matthew, Chapter 19. I like the New English Bible which reads: " 'If you wish to go the whole way, go, sell your possessions . . . and come follow me' " Chapter 19. And the young man upon hearing this was much cast down, ". . . he went away sorrowful . . ." Chapter 19.

No man can serve two masters and he chose the tinsel master of temporal riches instead of God's priceless eternal riches. A horrible choice! It's still being made by foolish men today.

IDOLATRY

In our country today there are few actual idols fashioned by men to worship as of old. God hated idols for they diverted the very love and fellowship that He created us to give to Him alone. He called idolatry and false religions harlotry. Anything that casts a shadow across our relationship with God is idolatry and we still have an abundance of it today.

These militate against a prosperous relationship with the Lord. Some of the kinds of things that stand in the way of our full relationship with God are everyday things that *overly* preoccupy us. Things that creep in to take His place . . . things such as our business, television, golf, bridge, camping, clothes, the house, family, mates, our denomination, the club. Do you see it? Beware of false gods that are always trying to enter your life.

THE FAT FARMER

"And he said unto them, Take heed, and beware of covetousness: for a man's life consisteth not in the abundance of the things which he possesseth." And he spake a parable unto them, saying, The ground of a certain rich man brought forth plentifully: And he thought within himself, saying, What shall I do, because I have no room where to bestow my fruits? And he said, This will I do: I will pull down my barns, and build greater; and there will I bestow all my fruits and my goods. And I will say to my soul, Soul, thou hast much goods laid up for many years; take thine ease, eat, drink, and be merry. But God said unto him, Thou fool, this night thy soul shall be required of thee: then whose shall those things be, which thou hast provided? So is he that layeth up treasure for himself, and is not rich toward God" Luke, Chapter 12.

Relevant searing truth and in such a few words!

The emphasis is on things. In Jesus' introduction to the parable we hear, ". . . A man's life consisteth not in the abundance of the things which he possesseth . . ." Chapter 12, and it is finalized with the words, ". . . then whose shall those *things* be . . ." Chapter 12.

This farmer isn't under some cloud of divine disapproval just because he owned a piece of fertile land and worked it well. He wasn't frowned on by God because he was successful in the things of the world.

Judgment struck because he was so completely *self*-centered. He was utterly oblivious to the claims of God on his life and wealth. He forgot that it was God who gave him life and the power to get that wealth. He obviously gave nothing back.

He didn't even acknowledge the Lord of the harvest in his gains. He had no consideration for anyone but *himself*. Notice that in these few verses the farmer uses the personal pronoun *I* eleven times!

This man was seething with the pride of life. He was a man who had ". . . gone in the way of Cain . . ." Jude. Cain, on being questioned about the welfare of his brother Abel, smarted off to God, "I know not: Am I my brother's keeper" Genesis, Chapter 4?

Also, the spirit of this farmer was like King Nebuchadnezzar of Babylon. In Daniel we learn that the great king took a walk one day, and surveyed the splendor of his kingdom and all his accomplishments. His head began to swell until he lost all perspective. Hear his boastful words, "Is not this great Babylon, that I have built for the house of the kingdom by the might of my power, and for the honour of my majesty" Daniel, Chapter 4?

The voice of divine judgment was heard from heaven and in that very hour his kingdom was taken from him.

God, upon whom Nebuchadnezzar was dependent for his every breath, relieved him of his reasoning power for seven years. He was dramatically shown on whom his life and prosperity depended. With God he was mighty—without Him, a fool grazing with his cattle.

Nebuchadnezzar was fortunate in that he was granted a reprieve so that we might have the benefit of his lesson. Nebuchadnezzar made a comeback. Not so the *self-confident* cocky farmer. We've all felt the spirit of that farmer rise up in us at some time of achievement. When we next feel this swelling self-pride come up in our breast we should remember these Bible personalities and give thanks to our Lord of the harvest. May God help us to remember in victory that all good things come from Him.

The Lord won't mind prospering you if He sees that it won't sicken your soul and separate you from Him.

13

RICH MAN, POOR MAN

We are rationed only a measured number of opportunities to demonstrate our understanding of divine stewardship in this life. We are tested by God on our material possessions and have only a set number of times to pass His tests. We never know just how soon we may exhaust our personal supply of opportunities as stewards. And that is what we are; merely caretakers of all things entrusted to us. We mustn't forget who it is that has title to those hills and their cattle.

What does God have to say on this theme?

"Will a man rob God? Yet ye have robbed me. But ye say, wherein have we robbed thee? In tithes and offerings. Ye are cursed with a curse: For ye have robbed me, even this whole nation. Bring ye all the tithes into the storehouse, that there may be meat in mine house, and prove me now herewith, saith the Lord of hosts, if I will not open you the window of heaven, and pour you out a blessing, that there shall not be room enough to receive it" Malachi, Chapter 3.

Have you demonstrated your generosity toward God and your dependability in even the tiny things so that He can safely prosper you as yet?

"He that is faithful in that which is least is faithful also in much: and he that is unjust in the least is unjust also in much. If therefore ye have not been faithful in the unrighteous mammon, who will commit to your trust the true riches? And if ye have not been faithful in that which is another man's, who shall give you that which is your own" Luke, Chapter 16?

Have you learned to give generously that you may qualify as a good vessel for God to prosper?

"Well, as you are eminent in everything, in faith and speech and knowledge and all zeal, and in your love for us, see that this beneficent spirit also flourishes in you" 2 Corinthians, Chapter 8 (WEYMOUTH).

There is no indication given that the rich farmer ever gave a thought to those about him who were in need. Moreover he never recognized the claims of God on his life and possessions. In regard to God's laws—ignorance is no defense. He has seen to it that Bibles are waiting everywhere to be read. We are all acquainted with a person like that farmer—perhaps a friend, a business partner, or a churchman. But how is it with you? Are *you* generous toward God and others? Do you have enough spiritual integrity as yet for God to work through you?

The hour came when that farmer had finally used up all his opportunities to pass this test. He flunked it, and life itself! "Thou fool, this night thy soul shall be required of thee . . ." Luke, Chapter 12.

No room was left for argument, nor for his explanation. Talkative men are speechless before God. "So is he that layeth up treasure for himself, and is not rich toward God" Chapter 12.

Before leaving our research on rich men, let's consider one more, for it is awesome with revelation. Jesus said: "There was a certain rich man, which was clothed in purple and fine linen, and fared sumptuously every day: And there was a certain beggar named Lazarus, which was laid at his gate, full of sores, And desiring to be fed with the crumbs which fell from the rich man's table: moreover the dogs came and licked his sores. And it came to pass, that the beggar died, and was carried by the angels into Abraham's bosom: the rich man also died, and was buried: And in hell he lift up his eyes, being in torments, and seeth Abraham afar off, and Lazarus in his bosom. And he cried and said, Father Abraham, have mercy on me, and send Lazarus, that he may dip the tip of his finger in water, and cool my tongue; for I am tormented in this flame. But Abraham said, Son, remember that thou in thy lifetime receivedst thy good things, and likewise Lazarus evil things: but now he is comforted, and thou art tormented. And beside all this, between us and you there is a great gulf fixed: so that they which would pass from hence to you cannot; neither can they pass to us, that would come from thence. Then he said, I pray thee therefore, father, that thou wouldest send him to my father's house: For I have five brethren; that he may testify unto them, lest they also come into this place of torment. Abraham saith unto him, They have Moses and the prophets; let them hear them. And he said, Nay, father Abraham; but if one went unto them from the dead, they will repent. And he said unto him, If they hear not Moses and the prophets, neither will they be persuaded, though one rose from the dead" Luke, Chapter 16.

Jesus didn't speak this as a parable nor an allegory. Nor was it a hypothetical situation, but a true story.

A *parable* is defined as being the comparison of two objects for the purpose of teaching. This method was employed by Jesus more than any other. He used the parable because it was an effective method of revealing truth to the spiritual and ready mind, and at the same time, of concealing it from the most intellectual but spiritually dark mind. Those who reject Jesus are not to even know the mysteries of the kingdom of heaven.

To speak in allegory is to set forth one thing in the image of another, so that the principal subject is inferred from the figure rather than by direct statement.

But there's nothing left to inference in the Lazarus report. Every item is set forth in high fidelity for even the spiritually dumb to hear.

This rich man was "clothed in purple." Purple was such an expensive dye that it was a mark of distinction to wear a purple robe. It was for royalty and high society. The "fine linen" came from Egypt, and it was also a symbol of wealth.

Ah, it's too often human tendency to clothe ourselves in purple and fine linen just to gain men's approval. But it's the wardrobe of the spirit that sets our position for eternity. Garments without spot or wrinkle are the garments of light.

Listen to the words of the Psalmist: "Be not thou afraid when one is made rich, when the glory of his house is increased; For when he dieth he shall carry nothing away: his glory shall not descend after him. Though while he lived he blessed his soul: and men will praise thee, when thou doest well to thyself. Man that is in honour, and understandeth not, is like the beasts that perish" Psalms, Chapter 49.

Just before the account of the rich man and Lazarus, Jesus had said to the Pharisees: "Ye are they which justify yourselves before men; but God knoweth your hearts: for that which is highly esteemed among men is abomination in the sight of God" Luke, Chapter 16.

This pompous and self-serving person whose name according to tradition was Dives, had lived it up with little regard for others or even for his own afterlife. He ate on this earth daily from a gourmet table, while ignoring a hungry cripple right outside his door. Heinous as this social sin was, it still wasn't the main reason for his doom. Nor was he in that place of torment as punishment for having been rich. He was there because through his lifetime with all its opportunities, he (like his elegant brothers left at home) had completely neglected to hear Moses and the prophets. If he had done so Godly charity would have become evident in his ways. There had been no time, no hunger, nor inclination to hear the voice of God—no desire to be reconciled with his Maker. He was a creature of time, but dead to eternity. His business no doubt kept him too busy to tune in on God . . . and he was too smart to believe in that life-after-death stuff. Sound familiar?

In each of these episodes involving people of wealth who failed God's test, there is a common denominator. The crux of each situation is not just in the fact that they were remiss in social action. It was their insensitivity to God's Word.

When the heart is open to God and His Word, when one encounters the grace of God through Jesus (as Zacchaeus did), all the other attributes of love and interest in one's fellow man blossom.

It's small wonder God warns that riches can be a snare and that it is as hard for a rich man to enter the Kingdom of Heaven as for a camel to pass through the eye of a needle. It's a nearly irresistible temptation for the rich to make a god of their money.

Good works, unless done as a result of divine concern, are still not going to be credited to our account, no matter how good our intentions. For "though I bestow all my goods to feed the poor, and though I give my body to be burned, and have not charity, ["God's love in me"; AMPLIFIED] I am nothing" 1 Corinthians, Chapter 13.

And God credits no gift from an unregenerate heart. (Remember Cain's spurned gift?) Giving must be an act of thanksgiving and worship. God reads our hearts more than our words and deeds. He tells us, "And whatsoever ye do in word or deed, do all in the name of the Lord Jesus, giving thanks to God and the Father by him" Colossians, Chapter 3.

14

THE CHRISTIAN FORTUNE COOKIE

Jesus had a lot to say about the spirit of giving and how to make it a rewarding part of worship. In the celebrated Sermon on the Mount Jesus said: "Take heed that ye do not your alms before men, to be seen of them: otherwise ye have no reward of your Father which is in heaven. Therefore when thou doest thine alms, do not sound a trumpet before thee, as the hypocrites do in the synagogues and in the streets, that they may have glory of men. Verily I say unto you, They have their reward. But when thou doest alms, let not thy left hand know what thy right hand doeth: That thine alms may be in secret: and thy Father which seeth in secret himself shall reward thee openly" Matthew, Chapter 6.

That old practice of fanfare sounds ludicrous but human nature has remained pretty much unchanged through the centuries. The appetite for approval and self-credit remains. There are more subtle and sophisticated ways of making sure that the left hand knows openly what the right hand is doing in our culture. The temptation to do this must be resisted or we won't be storing up those treasures after all.

One day Jesus sat down by the temple almsbox and watched the people as they put in their money. Many put in large offerings. "Then a poor widow came up and dropped in two little coins, together worth about a halfpenny. Jesus called his disciples to his side and said to them: 'Believe me, this poor widow has put in more than all the others. For they have all put in what they can easily spare, but she in her poverty who needs so much, has given away everything, her whole living' " Mark, Chapter 12 (PHILLIPS).

It seems that Jesus knows not only how much we give, but also how much we have left. He reads our bank balance and our attitude as well as our donation.

There was one act of love in giving that was so exemplary that all four of the Gospel writers recorded it (Matthew, Chapter 26, Mark, Chapter 14, Luke, Chapter 7 and John, Chapter 12). This was the occasion when Mary of Bethany used her alabaster jar of costly spikenard to anoint Jesus' head and feet. Now some, when they saw this were very indignant, and shook their heads, grumbling. They were of the group that still operates today. They wouldn't have wasted the oil on worthless emotional worship.

Those same are still pained to see so much expenditure on the intangible gospel. They want more budget going to the "relevant" things—crusades for social action to fight the here and now instead of spiritual crusades impacting eternity.

The Bible is candid in telling us that the one who led the protest concerning the woman with the precious ointment was a thief who really didn't care about the poor. Jesus loved Mary's sacrificial worship. It was relevant to Him. The very purpose for which we were created was for worship of and fellowship with God. Let's upgrade worship to Christ's perspective. It's not a minor component of our spiritual structure. It's the heart of it.

In a recent national magazine there was an article chiding some ministers for not giving a balanced presentation of Christian stewardship. The magazine writer criticized some ministers for misleading their people. He wrote about what he called a "prosperity plan" and says: "With these schemes comes the implied promise that such giving virtually guarantees the donor health and prosperity—a raise in pay or a better job." This may be too harsh an indictment, but God's truths for any area of life are like a well-cut gem with many sparkling facets. For us to overfocus on a single facet will give a biased slant on God's whole truth. In fact it distorts a truth if overdone. We are to give to God's work out of love for Him and not just to receive. God doesn't respond to an act of shaking a single verse in His face without considering His entire counsel.

Now, we don't want to criticize here those ministries that are teaching victory through *faith* in God's Word. For centuries there has been too little taught on this electrifying aspect of the Scriptures. There has been too much defeat in the guise of "I guess it's just God's will that I should be battered by Satan." These ministers are to be commended for restoring these victory truths through application of God's Word.

This reminds me of the "promise-box" theology. Now, I hope I don't spoil something dear to you, but come along anyway. During the first couple of years after I became a Christian, the promise-box selection was exciting. It was milk for this new babe.

After a little more time in my Bible, however, I began to see a faint distortion in that box idea. It began to look a bit like a Christian fortune cookie. I wondered if sales for the promise boxes might not suffer if they were stuffed with *all* of God's promises and not just certain ones.

Could you rejoice equally if you pulled one of *these* promises out of your box tomorrow morning?

". . . tribulation worketh patience" Romans, Chapter 5.

". . . though now for a season, if need be, ye are in heaviness through manifold temptations. . . ." 1 Peter, Chapter 1.

"But rejoice, inasmuch as ye are partakers of Christ's sufferings . . ." Chapter 4.

"As it is appointed unto men once to die, but after this the judgment" Hebrews, Chapter 9.

Do you see it? *All* of God's promises are valid and needful to the believer. The fiddler who plays one string brings forth no harmony. The Christian who harps on only part of God's revelation, plays an imperfect melody. This applies to prosperity plans as well as promise boxes.

Balanced truth is essential to our development as mature and strong Christians. Those fed on a diet of only the "sugary" blessings won't be as prepared to meet times of crisis. The whole counsel of God equips Christians for even the hardest trials that life can bring.

Teaching the give-and-get-rich idea without teaching, "For whom the Lord loveth he chasteneth . . ." Hebrews, Chapter 12, can build up a vulnerability. Teaching, "something good is going to happen today," without also teaching these "goodies" which were a part of mighty Paul's life, is less than the full gospel.

". . . in labours more abundant, in stripes above measure, in prisons more frequent, in deaths oft. Of the Jews five times received I forty stripes save one. Thrice was I beaten with rods, once was I stoned, thrice I suffered shipwreck, a night and a day I have been in the deep; In journeyings often, in perils of waters, in perils of robbers, in perils by mine own countrymen, in perils by the heathen, in perils in the city, in perils in the wilderness, in perils in the sea, in perils among false brethren; In weariness and painfulness, in watchings often, In hunger and thirst, in fastings often, in cold and nakedness" 2 Corinthians, Chapter 11.

Even though John the Apostle wrote to Gaius, "Beloved, I wish above all things that thou mayest prosper and be in health, even as thy soul prospereth" 3 John, it is equally true that we are not to try to make bargains with God. No shaking those promises under God's nose. Paul exclaims, ". . . who hath first given to him, and it shall be recompensed unto him again? For of him, and through him, and to him, are all things . . ." Romans, Chapter 11.

He was voicing by the Spirit what Job of ancient time learned when he heard the voice of Jehovah thunder these words, "Who has given to me, that I should repay him? Whatever is under the whole heaven is mine" Job, Chapter 41 (RSV).

This was a truth David often voiced in words like these: "But who am I, and what is my people, that we should be able thus to offer willingly? For all things come from thee, and of thy own have we given thee (1 Chronicles 29:14), and, "For the earth is the Lord's and the fullness thereof" 1 Corinthians, Chapter 10.

To teach that we can sort of force God's hand to give wealth is a shaky position. Following this tack produces an imbalance and when bounty doesn't rain many are apt to become mighty discouraged Christians. God rewards His children in His own way and in His own time and with His own coin. God—He is God!

This surely isn't to say that it is the will of God for any of His children to be forever on the verge of poverty. But many saints through centuries of church history could identify with Peter and John when they said to the beggar at the Gate Beautiful "Silver and gold have I none . . ." Acts, Chapter 3. God certainly wasn't at enmity with Peter and John, was He? They continued however and spent of the coin in which they were rich, "In the name of Jesus Christ of Nazareth rise up and walk" Chapter 3.

Jesus says, "Hearken, my beloved brethren, Hath not God chosen the poor of this world rich in faith, and heirs of the kingdom which he hath promised to them that love him" James, Chapter 2?

There is no intent in exposing this other side of Bible doctrine to imply that people who receive salvation should resign themselves to a lifetime of penury, want and deprivation. Not at all! Both sides of God's coin are His. God's whole coin is richer than half. It better prepares us to maintain the attitude of peace and unswerving trust that Paul showed in stating, ". . . I have learned, in whatsoever state I am, therewith to be content" Philippians, Chapter 4. *Therein* lies our secret of peace and prosperity of soul in this life. Now that didn't hurt so badly after all, did it?

Kenneth Copeland says that prosperity is no accident. It is governed by physical and spiritual laws that are revealed in the Word of God. Anyone attempting to study these laws must first have a proper definition of true prosperity. The world's definition of prosperity is primarily *monetary affluence*. But spiritual prosperity would include the ability to invoke God's power to meet the needs of other people.

God's power not only includes the ability to meet a person's needs financially but also his needs spiritually, mentally, and physically. God's power covers a vast area that financial power alone can never cover.

Now a man that is truly prosperous is a man that has not only the ability to believe in God for his own financial needs, but also knows how to exercise faith to meet the needs of other people. This would, for example, include the area of sickness where at times money is insufficient.

God's power is the highest, greatest, and most far-reaching in this universe. *Faith* is the bridge between that power and us. This faith can only be realized by acting on the Word. It is sovereign and will reach beyond the outer limits of financial power.

It is written "For the word of God is . . . sharper than any twoedged sword, piercing even to the dividing asunder of soul and spirit, and of the joints and marrow, and is a discerner of the thoughts and intents of the heart" Hebrews, Chapter 4. That covers the spectrum of human existence!

We have seen in years past that no political power can stop the Word of God. It can momentarily deter, but never stop. Even atheistic communism hasn't been able to stop it. When a person acts on God's Word, he has touched the power of God and God's Word begins to work. We must place God's Word in *first* place in our lives. We must learn to act on it as confidently as we would on the word of a trusted lawyer, doctor, or our wisest friend. This is the first step toward true prosperity.

We are the extension of God's power in this world. As we act on the Word of God we can become God's channel to meet needs of others. The world believes that the highest form of power is money, but prayer is the highest. If we pray and act in harmony with God's Word we are linked by faith to the highest power that exists. This enables us to be used in meeting the needs of other people. God has given us the power to love even the most destitute, and through faith in His Word the opportunity to do something about it.

15

CHRISTMAS EVERY DAY

In the beginning—God.

Standing in the brilliance of God's love shining on humanity, everything that we can do for Him pales to insignificance. One of Jesus' parables concluded, "So likewise ye, when ye shall have done all those things which are commanded you, say, We are unprofitable servants: we have done that which was our duty to do" Luke, Chapter 17.

God so loved the world that he disrupted heaven to send down His Son, and by that Son all benefits are continually pouring upon His children. Let's check on just a few of our benefits:

True bread: Jesus said, ". . . my Father giveth you the true bread from heaven" John, Chapter 6.

Good things: "If ye then, being evil, know how to give good gifts unto your children, how much more shall your Father which is in heaven give good things to them that ask him" Matthew, Chapter 7?

Life, breath, all things: Paul declared on Mar's hill, "Neither is God worshipped with men's hands, as though he needed anything, seeing he giveth to all life, and breath, and all things" Acts, Chapter 17.

Love of God: And he wrote to the Romans, ". . . the love of God is shed abroad in our hearts by the Holy Ghost which is given unto us" Romans, Chapter 5.

All things: "He that spared not his own Son, but delivered him up for us all, how shall he not with him also freely give us all things" Chapter 8.

Increase: Paul wrote the Corinthians that when any minister enjoys a harvest in his work it is God that gives the increase. (See 1 Corinthians, Chapter 3.)

Victory: And that even death's sting is removed, and the grave has no victory because God has given us the victory over the grave through Jesus. (See 1 Corinthians, Chapter 15.)

Good and perfect gifts: James states positively, "Every good gift and every perfect gift is from above, and cometh down from the Father of lights . . ." James, Chapter 1.

Wisdom: He further promises the sorely needed gift of wisdom ". . . ask of God that giveth to all men liberally, and upbraideth not; and it shall be given him" Chapter 1.

Life and godliness: God's divine power through Jesus has given us "all things that pertain unto life and godliness" 2 Peter, Chapter 1, not necessarily all the material things that the family across the street has, but things much more valuable—real things pertaining to the more abundant life, and things money can never buy.

Great promises: Also there are given unto us ". . . exceeding great and precious promises: that by these we might be partakers of the divine nature . . ." 2 Peter, Chapter 1. Just think of it? All bought at the cross and free to God's children.

Gifts and fruit of the Spirit: Then there is the magnificent basket of the gifts and fruit of the Spirit. As we stand in awe of these, and so many more which God gives us, we cry with Paul, "Thanks be unto God for his unspeakable gift" 2 Corinthians, Chapter 9!

Do you realize that you are actually richer than Midas, Howard Hughes, Paul Getty and all the Rockefellers put together?

Somewhere—before design for the world was finished—when the plan of the ages was being worked out, God's Son volunteered for the most awesome role ever played. When He came to earth to fulfill that commitment He reconfirmed it saying, "Lo, I come to do thy will, O God" Hebrews, Chapter 10.

"Who verily was foreordained before the foundation of the world, but was manifest in these last times for you" 1 Peter, Chapter 1. This song expresses the idea: "Out of the Ivory Palaces, Into a world of woe."

And Jesus made good! He came expressly to give. "He gave Himself as a ransom for many." That ransom affects every phase of life. Yes, Christmas every day now and forever.

HE THOUGHT OF EVERYTHING

The world today seems more concerned than ever before about certain problems. From every media our eyes and ears are assaulted with many "in" words. Prominent among them are: PEACE, POVERTY, LOVE, TRUTH, DISEASE, LABOR, SECURITY, ECOLOGY and POLLUTION.

They scream "Something must be done!" The truth is that something has been done. Jesus came to meet these problems head on for us. As long as we honored Him and followed His Word we prospered, but increasingly we have crisis in each of these areas as we have drifted from His provisions.

PEACE: He said, "Peace I leave with you, my peace I give unto you . . . Let not your heart be troubled, neither let it be afraid" John, Chapter 14. We lack peace because we dishonor the Prince of Peace!

LOVE: Singers croon, "What the world needs now is love, sweet love. . . ." Many who sing it, really mean "lust, sweet lust." More true love has already been offered to the world than it has received. "Greater love hath no man than this, that a man lay down his life for his friends" John, Chapter 15.

TRUTH: So often today a confused world reechoes Pilate's question, "What is truth" John, Chapter 18? Jesus' answer was, "I am . . . the truth" Chapter 14!

John said, "And the Word was made flesh, and dwelt among us, (and we beheld his glory, the glory as of the only begotten of the Father,) full of grace and truth" Chapter 1.

The placard carriers march and shout for truth and freedom while Jesus offers, "And ye shall know the truth, and the truth shall make you free" Chapter 8.

SECURITY: Is security possible in such a reeling, chaotic world? Listen to John's fascinating account of an insecure person Jesus met one day by a well. Jesus, looking into her very soul, knew her need and drew her into a conversation. He shared truth with her. He reminded her that all who drink of the world's water just become thirsty again. "But whosoever drinketh of the water that I shall give him shall be in him a well of water springing up into everlasting life" Chapter 4. What a promise!

Never ending security for her thirsty soul! The life of this woman, and that of many of her friends, was *forever secured*. They took of His eternal safety when He offered not only the water of life, but also the bread of heaven.

"And Jesus said unto them, I am the bread of life: he that cometh to me shall never hunger; and he that believeth on me shall never thirst" John, Chapter 6.

Then the ultimate in safety and power during this lifetime, ". . . whom the world cannot receive . . ."—is the gift of the Comforter, the gift of the Holy Spirit which our Lord gives to His own. Unshakeable comfort for time, and security for eternity, to every believer. Truly we are rich beyond measure.

DISEASE: Jesus went about doing good and healing those that were oppressed of the devil.

Luke writes of a day Jesus stood on a great plain. Thousands from Judea and Jerusalem and from the seacoast towns of Tyre and Sidon came to hear Him and to seek remedy. "And the whole multitude sought to touch him: for there went virtue out of him, and healed them all" Luke, Chapter 6.

Luke also tells us of a poor, incurably ill woman who pressed her way through and touched just the edge of Jesus' clothing and was *instantly* healed. Jesus said "Somebody hath touched me: for I perceive that virtue is gone out of me" Luke, Chapter 8.

Jesus gives of the very *essence of Himself*. One of His great names is Physician. The fee was paid by Himself as those lashes were taken on His back. ". . . by whose stripes ye were healed" 1 Peter, Chapter 2. Many of His children daily turn their backs on this same Great Physician today.

POVERTY: Some man may say, "But what did Jesus do about the poverty problem?" It has been one of the curses of the human race since the fall in Eden. It is a universal problem brought on by spiritual rebellion which gave Satan this temporary world dominion. But it has a solution.

"He became poor, in order that by His poverty you might

become enriched—abundantly supplied" 2 Corinthians, Chapter 8 (AMPLIFIED).

Amazing grace indeed!

We may be accused of being simplistic about difficulties that have plagued the world since Satan's rise. But the world has never tried *His* solutions! All Christians who have tried Him have learned his promise is really true, "But God shall supply all your need according to his riches in glory by Christ Jesus" Philippians, Chapter 4. We shall see all this displayed worldwide as Christ reigns in the soon-coming millennium.

LABOR: Jesus invites every straining human, "Come unto me, all ye that labour and are heavy laden, and I will give you rest. Take my yoke upon you, and learn of me; for I am meek and lowly in heart: and ye shall find rest unto your souls" Matthew, Chapter 11. This is God's answer to the weariness of sweating humanity.

But we must act on his promises. They aren't automatic. He doesn't force His blessings on us. We have free will to ignore ALL His solutions.

ECOLOGY and POLLUTION: There is a furor today regarding these particular "in" words. Pollution and litter are just the tracks of fallen mankind. God built in magnificent recirculating, self-cleansing and automatic healing for the water and land. This planet was fearfully and wonderfully designed for our enjoyment. But it wasn't built to remain pure for eternal abuse by sin-damned, destructive humankind.

Our urgent ecology crisis underscores and highlights the fact that our earth is nearing the end of its utility. This global fouling may be retarded, but it cannot be reversed until Christ returns. Our all-knowing, long-range-planning Creator long ago planned the ultimate ecological solution. It's been right there in the Word all along: ". . . a new heaven and a new earth . . ." Revelation, Chapter 21. Won't that be something!

A far greater ecology crisis is raging in the hearts of men than in the streams of earth. God will in time renew the earth, but we must fight now against the pollution of men's souls. Man is being fatally poisoned with pornography, hate, the occult, immorality and alienation from God. This is the pollution battleground on which we are to war against Satan, the archcorrupter. But the blood of Jesus is the superdetergent that can reverse our pollution against God.

What lessons to be learned from God's Word! All have a bearing on every contemporary problem. No human need was overlooked by our designer—the Author and Finisher.

THE ULTIMATE GIVER

There was a missionary girl who was serving some ten years ago in a hot backward country. It got so tough she despaired of her life. The climate was unendurable, the customs of the people repugnant and the language impossible. The insects plagued her and the animals frightened her. The people to whom she had gone with high hopes were not only unresponsive but utterly indifferent.

In a surge of rebellion she said, "I don't have to stay here! I'm going back home to work among those who care." The next day she was putting her plan into action. As she was busily packing she heard a voice she knew! Speaking gently, He said, "But I came much farther for your sake."

That was enough. She unpacked. Yes, there was One who was willing to come—eons away! And He even became poor for us. Our customs were anything but pleasant for Him. Men's hearts were filled with uncleanness, and it erupted before Him in their speech and in their deeds. He too hated disease and infirmity. But He warred over it. They were indifferent about His visit too. He cast devils from the demoniac and in return was asked to leave town.

"He came unto his own, and his own received him not" John, Chapter 1. He was reviled and lied about. But He came to give— and stayed until He had given.

He *gave* His face to shame and spitting and to those that plucked off the hair. He *gave* His back to the smiters; and finally His life. He said, "No man taketh it from me, but I lay it down of myself" John, Chapter 10.

But that wasn't the end—it was only the beginning. . . . Because of *His* giving come all benefits and all our blessings. In the light of such giving, by Jesus the Son of God, how can any of us feel we've given enough? Every gift we now give will be such an ecstasy as He sits down to savor each one with us soon. That judgment of our works can be such a bright day if we choose!

16

FOLLOW THE LEADER

More than a few have been willing to give all for His cause, and the list is still growing. Only a few can be mentioned here, but all are known to God.

First there were the Apostles. When Peter said, "Lo, we have left all, and followed thee" Luke, Chapter 18, he wasn't boasting; neither was he complaining. He was stating a *fact,* and Jesus didn't dispute it.

After the death, burial, resurrection and ascension of Jesus, and after Pentecost, the list of those entering the Hall of Heavenly Fame grew. "And all that believed . . . sold their possessions and goods . . ." Acts, Chapter 2. (See also Acts, Chapter 4.)

The Bible says that there was a "multitude" of such totally dedicated contributors in the early church, but we only learn the name of one. (See Acts, Chapter 4.) There may have been a reason why Barnabas was singled out for mention.

According to historical writers, Barnabas was by today's standards a millionaire. It must have shaken up the business community when they heard that Barnabas had gone all the way; and that he too had given all of his possessions to the cause of Jesus.

Those in that early church were led by the Holy Spirit to liquidate their holdings and give the proceeds to the spreading of the gospel. They were also led to get their bags packed for their trip and thus Barnabas's obedience kept his wealth from being wasted. Barnabas didn't know that in A.D. 70 all the Jews would be kicked out of Israel because of Titus's decree. We too must get ready for our soon-coming "trip." It's imperative we do not become encumbered or earthbound. Ours will be a more pleasant trip than that of the early church. Ours will be a literal High Adventure with the King!

We have in our country a number of so-called first families. The progenitors of these families began to build fortunes in their day, from such enterprises as lumber, shipping, mining, railroading, and land. This was before the day of heavy taxes. Great fortunes were amassed, great mansions built, and there was wide acquisition of properties. Many have been passed down from one generation to the next.

For the sake of supposition: should the head of one of these rich families become an ardent follower of Christ—even to the extent of selling off his huge wealth and donating everything to Christian works, we would soon read it in *Time* and *Newsweek*.

Many in the early church adopted communal living and put all their possessions in for the common cause. Some ask whether this isn't the living pattern most pleasing to God. There have been communal groups throughout church history. And they've started up again in our time. We believe, however, this was unique for that early church. It has worked poorly since. We see no divine command that all believers should pool things in common. However, there was a reason for this Spirit-directed move for the early church, as subsequent events proved. God's Spirit knew that violent Roman storms of persecution were soon to descend on the church and that Christians would be uncoupled from their lands and holdings by Titus.

James begins his epistle: "James, a servant of God and of the Lord Jesus Christ, unto the twelve tribes which are scattered abroad . . ." James, Chapter 1.

And Peter addresses his letter: "to the strangers" [or sojourners of the dispersion] scattered throughout Pontus, Galatia, Cappadocia, Asia, and Bithynia, 1 Peter, Chapter 1.

How thankful these sojourners must have been that they could at least know before it was too late, that their giving had counted for the gospel. Knowing that their properties, houses and "bank accounts" had largely gone to the cause of Christ. The proceeds had already helped launch Christianity. "The steps of a good man are ordered by the Lord . . ." Psalms, Chapter 37. Should our generation of believers prepare? We too are approaching an exodus—the rapture. The mood is set by the songwriter:

Child of my Love, fear not the unknown morrow,
Dread not the new demand life makes of thee;
Thy ignorance doth hold no cause for sorrow—
Since what thou knowest not is known to Me.

It wasn't just human exhortation that moved those early believers in regard to their money. Let's take another look at that puzzling episode involving Ananias and Sapphira, his wife.

Perhaps they wanted to appear generous, but feared to trust all the way. Whatever the reason, they sold a piece of their land and kept back a part of the proceeds as a nest egg, against the urging of the Holy Spirit. They brought a big portion of it to church and put it in the collection with the pretense that they had brought it *all*. Their action seems at first glance to have been generous, but it brought immediate and catastrophic judgment! Both were stricken dead and buried within hours.

This fearful episode would indicate that it was the privilege of Ananias and Sapphira to do as they pleased with their own property. They still had free will. Their lethal sin had been in lying to God. They had brought a falsehood into the holy place and before their Christian brethren. God had looked upon their hearts and what they withheld from Him, as well as upon their gift. This lesson is still relevant today. God doesn't write any irrelevant matters in the Bible. Note also that Sapphira was judged even though she acted under Ananias's urging.

There was still another problem in the days when Israel was under the leadership of Joshua. It happened back when God's people were fighting in Canaan for their promised possession. They were exhilarated by an unbroken string of tremendous victories. Province after province, city after city, had fallen into their hands—even impregnable Jericho.

"So the Lord was with Joshua; and his fame was noised throughout all the country" Joshua, Chapter 6. But, right in the midst of this string of victories something terrible happened! Israel went to battle one day flushed with faith but they were suddenly clobbered by the puny forces of Ai. Joshua's army was routed in confusion and dismay by little Ai.

What suddenly turned their invincibility to whimpering weakness?

Well, it was such a "little" thing! *One man* out of the army's thousands had secretly disobeyed explicit orders given to Joshua by the Lord for this time. One soldier was tempted to take some of the beautiful heathen spoil since no man would ever know. By his own admission, Achan said, ". . . I coveted them, and took them; and behold, they are hid in the earth in the midst of my tent . . ." Chapter 7.

Because of this one man's sin of disobedience, covetousness and deceit, the whole timetable of Israel suffered terribly. God is a holy, righteous God, yet we try to compromise with Him constantly in little things. He's never changed! We are holding back God's final victory today by our own covetousness. We too are obeying our flesh instead of our God.

The cause of Christ is still harmed, and the church often brought to confusion and impotence, because of hidden deep sins of some members of the body.

"Now all these things happened unto them for ensamples: and they are written for our admonition, upon whom the ends of the world are come" 1 Corinthians, Chapter 10, wrote Peter. That Peter knew of what he wrote for he had attended Galilee Bible College under the professorship of Jesus Himself.

Just like Ananias and Sapphira, swift and terrible judgment came upon guilty Achan and his entire household. The saying "Cheaters never prosper," also goes for things of the Spirit.

Beloved, God is seeking channels through which He can now pour great sums for the completion of His work. He is ready to do it on a large scale where He can find trustworthy stewards. We have already seen this working in the lives of men in our time such as LeTourneau, Clement Stone, Art DeMoss, Demos Shakarian and many, many other faithful servants. At times God will start to prosper others and then have to withhold His hand of blessing as some are tempted to hold out on Him, or start to take the credit for themselves. This is dangerous.

We are told in Hebrews, Chapter 10, "It is a fearful thing to fall into the hands of the living God."

Contrariwise, it is delightful to remember that: "The mercy of the Lord is from everlasting to everlasting upon them that fear him, and his righteousness unto children's children; To such as keep his covenant, and to those that remember his commandments to do them" Psalms, Chapter 103.

But could it be that sometimes we emphasize the mercy of God so much that we forget that He is also a *Holy* God? He still can't excuse unrepented sins, even the little ones which we may have swept under the rug.

One of God's big spenders for the gospel's sake was Paul. He had been established both in the political and the ecclesiastical realm. He profited in the Jewish religion more than most. Paul was highly educated and a Hebrew of Hebrews.

But God is sovereign and it was His will to separate this proud and successful Jew unto the Gospel. So by unique means He dazzled Saul of Tarsus with His presence. He opened his heart to THE Truth which changed his nature. He finally even changed his name.

So what did this Paul do with all that fame and worth from his former life? Paul's encounter so motivated him that he gave his substance, all his personal dreams, and his life. Let him tell it: "But what things were gain to me, those I counted loss for Christ." And "I have suffered the loss of all things . . . that I may win for Christ" Philippians, Chapter 3.

He later wrote the Corinthians concerning himself and his fellow workers in the gospel: ". . . [We] have no certain dwelling-place; And labour, working with our own hands . . ." 1 Corinthians, Chapter 4.

To the Thessalonians: "For ye remember, brethren, our labour and travail: for labouring night and day, because we would not be chargeable unto any of you, we preached unto you the gospel of God" 1 Thessalonians, Chapter 2.

"Neither did we eat any man's bread for nought; but wrought with labour and travail night and day, that we might not be chargeable to any of you . . ." 2 Thessalonians, Chapter 3.

To his converts in Ephesus Paul said: "I have coveted no man's silver, or gold, or apparel. Yea, ye yourselves know, that these hands have ministered unto my necessities, and to them that were with me. I have shewed you all things, how that so labouring ye ought to support the weak, and to remember the words of the Lord Jesus, how he said, It is more blessed to give than to receive" Acts, Chapter 20.

Now this isn't to infer that all who serve the Lord should also make their own living. We've heard some say that all ministers should "work with their hands" as Paul did, and shouldn't accept any salary whatsoever from the church.

But let's hear Paul's words again: "Who goeth a warfare any time at his own charges? who planteth a vineyard, and eateth not of the fruit thereof? or who feedeth a flock, and eateth not of the milk of the flock? Say I these things as a man? or saith not the law the same also? For it is written in the law of Moses, Thou shalt not muzzle the mouth of the ox that treadeth out the corn. Doth God take care for oxen? Or saith he it altogether for our sakes? For our sakes, no doubt, this is written: that he that ploweth should plow in hope; and that he that thresheth in hope should be partaker of his hope. If we have sown unto you spiritual things, is it a great thing if we shall reap your carnal things? Do ye not know that they which minister about holy things live of the things of the temple? and they which wait at the altar are partakers with the altar? Even so hath the Lord ordained that they which preach the gospel should live of the gospel" 1 Corinthians, Chapter 9.

And to the Galatians Paul said: "The man under Christian instruction should be willing to contribute toward the livelihood of his teacher" Galatians, Chapter 6 (PHILLIPS).

Paul taught the Philippians about the profit in giving to a godly ministry. "As you know yourselves, Philippians, in the early days of my mission, when I set out from Macedonia, you alone of all our congregations were my partners in payments and receipts; for even at Thessalonica you contributed to my needs, not once but twice over. Do not think I set my heart upon the gift; all I care for is the profit accruing to you. However, here I give you my receipt for everything . . . I am paid in full, now that I have received from Epaphroditus what you sent. It is a fragrant offering, an acceptable sacrifice, pleasing to God." Philippians, Chapter 4 (NEB).

In the book of Timothy he taught the wealthy how to transfer their money to the high interest Bank of Heaven. "Charge them that are rich in this world, that they be not highminded, nor trust in uncertain riches, but in the living God, who giveth us richly all things to enjoy; That they do good, that they be rich in good works, ready to distribute, willing to communicate" 1 Timothy, Chapter 6.

In the Amplified Version of the Bible we read, "Do not forget or neglect . . . to be generous and distribute and contribute to the needy [of the church] . . ." Hebrews, Chapter 13.

In this same vein Paul told the Galatians: "As we have therefore opportunity, let us do good unto all men, especially unto them who are of the household of faith" Galatians, Chapter 6. It is especially pleasing to God that our affluency be shared with ministers and other Christians in need.

17

DIRTY FOUR-LETTER WORD

God wrote, "All scripture is given by inspiration of God, and is profitable for doctrine, for reproof, for correction, for instruction in righteousness" 2 Timothy, Chapter 3.

That is why Christians must "eat" heartily of the Bible, which is the food for our spirit. For it is by this heavenly food that our spirit grows. The Word of God is also the light for our life's path. It is essential that we be sensitive to dangers that begin to rise up in our midst.

There were certain attitudes of life which our nation formerly adhered to, and through which it became great—attitudes on such ideas as work, generosity, honesty and contentment.

Today new doctrines are being heard. Basic principles are under attack. Some foolish liberals, like termites from hell, are eating away at many of the structures which built this magnificent nation. These structures, built under the laws of God, have prospered our people. They have also made a place of refuge for the fearful, the unhappy, and the oppressed peoples of the world. Here such people have found a quality of life that has never been equaled in all history.

But now we are seeing fulfillment of the words of the Apostle Jude when he described certain ones as "filthy dreamers [who] defile the flesh, despise dominion, and speak evil of dignities" He said moreover, "But these speak evil of those things which they know not . . ." Jude.

Both Jude and Peter describe those whose mouths are full of "great swelling words." Paul, writing to Timothy also had these words of warning: "You must face the fact: the final age of this world is to be a time of troubles. Men will love nothing but money and self; they will be arrogant, boastful, and abusive; with no respect for parents, no gratitude, no piety, no natural affection; they will be implacable in their hatreds, scandalmongers, intemperate and fierce, strangers to all goodness, traitors, adventurers, swollen with self-importance" 2 Timothy, Chapter 3 (NEB).

Now how in the world could Paul, Peter and Jude have written such a perfect description of the troublemakers in our world today? They wrote, of course, by the Holy Spirit. He knows all things—past, present, and distant future.

Termites! They serve no useful purpose. They take but never give. They destroy but have no knowledge of how to build.

Yes, great swelling words! We now hear them regularly. Wealth is evil! Let future generations worry for themselves. We're the NOW generation. *Work* is a dirty four-letter word! "Better red than dead." Of our institutions, built with toil and sacrifice, "Burn them down!" "If it feels good, do it!" And one of the females of the tribe shouts, "It ain't a crime to murder—but it's a crime to own property!"

Volumes could be filled with their great swelling words. But let's hear what God has to say about some of the attitudes and activities that He knows are best for us.

It has been a while since God has been listened to by the world. Never in history has there been so much talk. Radios and talk programs, the press and lecterns, present the *world's* doctrines. But the treasure of God's wisdom lies patiently in the hundred million Bibles scattered through the land. One day it may be reawakened just as it was reawakened by the Israelites who rediscovered it under the dusty litter in the temple. Let's see what God has to say about that four-letter word—WORK:

"Be kindly affectioned one to another with brotherly love; in honour preferring one another; Not slothful in business; fervent in spirit; serving the Lord" Romans, Chapter 12.

"And that ye study to be quiet, and to do your own business, and to work with your own hands, as we commanded you; That ye may walk honestly toward them that are without, and that ye may have lack of nothing" 1 Thessalonians, Chapter 4.

"And withal they learn to be idle, wandering about from house to house; and not only idle, but tattlers also and busybodies, speaking things which they ought not" 1 Timothy, Chapter 5.

"But if any provide not for his own, and specially for those of his own house, he hath denied the faith, and is worse than an infidel" 1 Timothy, Chapter 5.

If men would now take these words to heart, the welfare crush on the weary taxpayers would shrink considerably.

"Let him that stole steal no more: but rather let him labour, working with his hands the thing which is good, that he may have to give to him that needeth" Ephesians, Chapter 4.

"Neither did we eat any man's bread for nought . . . for even when we were with you, this we commanded you, that if any would not work, neither should he eat. For we hear that there are some which walk among you disorderly, working not at all, but are busybodies. Now them that are such we command and exhort by our Lord Jesus Christ, that with quietness they work . . ." 2 Thessalonians, Chapter 3.

Lord Chesterfield, noted English statesman and author, wrote in a letter to his son: "I look upon indolence as a sort of suicide; for the man is effectually destroyed, though the appetites of the brute may survive."

Charles Dickens said that the first external revelations of the dry rot in men is a tendency to lurk and lounge; to be at street corners without intelligible reason.

Calvin Coolidge stated that work is not a curse; it is the prerogative of intelligence, the only means to manhood, and the measure of civilization.

We see today a frightening deterioration in our nation's sinews as God's laws on work are violated.

Selfish leaders are forcing exorbitantly high wages for less and less work. Our easy welfare has encouraged slothfulness and penalized the industrious tax-paying citizen.

Yes, we are breaking spiritual laws of work and industry. We are now in the process of being arrested. No wonder the alarming rise in our national debt and the deterioration in our international balances. We have priced our own goods right out of the world market. It is now reaping time for the tares sown in opposition to God's Word.

COVETOUSNESS: The law of love toward a neighbor is, "Thou shalt not covet" Romans, Chapter 13. Covetousness is a cyclone in the nation. Coveting that which has been earned by others is growing in popularity. It is becoming the political thing to promote this.

Paul lists it along with other gross sins: "Being filled with all unrighteousness, fornication, wickedness, covetousness, maliciousness; full of envy, murder, debate, deceit, malignity; whisperers" Chapter 1.

Jesus had already spoken to his followers: "And he said unto them, Take heed, and beware of covetousness: for a man's life consisteth not in the abundance of the things which he possesseth" Luke, Chapter 12. He was saying, "Watch out! Be on guard lest this ugly destructive thing gain a place in your heart."

"Mortify therefore your members which are upon the earth; fornication, uncleanness, inordinate affection, evil concupiscence, and covetousness, which is idolatry" Colossians, Chapter 3.

One of the earmarks of false teachers is covetousness. "And through covetousness shall they with feigned words make merchandise of you: whose judgment now of a long time lingereth not, and their damnation slumbereth not" 2 Peter, Chapter 2.

And finally, an admonition, coupled with a quotation from Christ Himself, giving warm assurance of His tender and everlasting care for His own. "Let your conversation be without covetousness; and be content with such things as ye have: for he hath said, I will never leave thee, nor forsake thee" Hebrews, Chapter 13.

DISHONESTY: Stealing, or theft was made the subject of one of the ten commandments, "Thou shalt not steal." It directly clashes with the present Satan-inspired "rip off." Jesus reminded the rich young ruler of His attitude toward dishonesty as He said to him, "Thou knowest the commandments, Do not commit adultery, Do not kill, Do not steal, Do not bear false witness, Defraud not, Honour thy father and mother" Mark, Chapter 10. Jesus considered those spiritual precepts as basic.

Paul wrote to the church in Ephesus: "Let him that stole steal no more: but rather let him labour, working with his hands the thing which is good, that he may have to give to him that needeth" Ephesians, Chapter 4.

The word by the Spirit to the Thessalonians was an admonition coupled with a warning which is for every businessman, housewife, laborer, and child. "That no man go beyond and defraud his brother in any matter: because that the Lord is the avenger of all such, as we also have forewarned you and testified" 1 Thessalonians, Chapter 4.

It would seem a time to reemphasize these warnings, for all things are naked and open unto the eyes of the Christ we shall soon encounter face to face. Many think they are getting away with subtle dishonesties here. They rationalize by saying, "Everyone I work with does it." Company time, stamps, phones. . . .

But there is a day of accounting. Nothing is hidden from Christ. Those who fail to keep their *secret* records clean will find the bitter truth of that same word. "It is a fearful thing to fall into the hands of the living God" Hebrews, Chapter 10.

Remember, we can steal in many different ways. We must examine our ways continually, for our own hearts are deceitful to us.

Tax fudging, delinquent household bills, unpaid tithes (stealing from God), time wasted on the job, cheating our mate, etc. God wants us to dress up quickly without spot or wrinkle. It's time to review with a critical eye all of our little practices in life. Will they stand the scrutiny of Jesus' eye? He wants to bless and honor honesty and righteousness. We must not inadvertently rob ourselves! Often it's those little foxes that spoil our vines.

We must also remember that God can't bless a Christian in businesses such as the liquor, nightclub or gambling business. He doesn't look at a man one way on Sunday and another on Monday. Neither will he brook questionable business methods anymore. After finding Christ many are faced with the task of cleaning up their lives and business practices, and some must even abandon their old work.

There are sad cases of men who have tried to straddle two worlds after conversion. Only chaos and heartbreak result.

LITIGATION: One of the tragedies of these end-times, is the collapsing of our system of justice. The news is filled with it. Criminals coddled, greedy lawyers, clogged court calendars, foolish judges, overworked police, legal confusion. . . .

This deterioration of the effectiveness and integrity of the legal system underscores the wisdom of God in this realm.

In *The Living Bible* we read: "How is it that when you have something against another Christian, you 'go to law,' and ask a heathen court to decide the matter instead of taking it to other

Christians to decide which of you is right? Don't you know that some day we Christians are going to judge and govern the world? So why can't you decide even these little things among yourselves? Don't you realize that we Christians will judge and reward the very angels in heaven? So you should be able to decide your problems down here on earth easily enough. Why then go to outside judges who are not even Christians? I am trying to make you ashamed. Isn't there anyone in all the church who is wise enough to decide these arguments? But instead one Christian sues another and accuses his Christian brother in front of unbelievers. To have such arguments at all is a real defeat for you as Christians. Why not just accept mistreatment and leave it at that? It would be far more honoring to the Lord to let yourself be cheated. But instead you yourselves are the ones who do wrong, cheating others, even your own brothers" 1 Corinthians, Chapter 6 (TLB).

Yes, it really is better to allow yourself to be taken than to get into litigation. Some Christians are disobedient in this area and find themselves enmeshed in this nerve-racking legal forest. It gives great pleasure to God's enemy to see Christians fighting and exposing the shame of other Christians. Why, they're doing *his* work!

I don't even recommend litigation for cases involving non-Christians anymore. Try to avoid at almost any cost the entanglements of the courts. The wear on nerves, the uncertainty of real justice, the attorney's costs and the great loss of time, speak against litigation today.

Remember too that we believers are deemed worthy to judge even the angels. Wouldn't we be safer then to entrust our case against another Christian to the least of the believers than to give it to even the greatest among the children of this world?

ENTERTAINMENT FOR GAIN: Some months after I became a Christian a new conviction began to grow in me about my business entertaining. For years I had taken for granted that it was a must in business to wine and dine my customers. This is a deeply entrenched business practice, worldwide—the expected thing. After awhile this began to bug me! It clashed with the Bible, and I began to think about phasing it out of my business. The very thought of this change really worried me. It seemed like such a dangerous move. I was sure it would cost us thousands and that we would lose our competitiveness in sales.

Then some months after I chopped it out I spilled my worries to a close customer friend who had been a recipient of our favors in the past.

He said, "George, let me put your mind at ease. Many of us buyers accept these boozing and partying nights on the town. In the cold light of dawn, however, we feel safer placing our business with fellows who don't carouse and on whom we can better depend to fill our contracts. Sometimes we glibly thank a fellow for partying us, but later resent that he has led us to play the fool! We don't like to lose our own self-respect either, you know."

It was a great practical sermon! I was frankly surprised to see that our own sales results actually *improved* after abandoning that practice. Going with God is never a sacrifice in business. It was a delightful discovery.

HONESTY: And the paying of debts. During the ministry of John the Baptist people with many different backgrounds and occupations came to hear this fiery, straight-talking preacher. Having heard, their consciences were pricked. Among these people were publicans, farmers, housewives and business people.

The gospel-writer gives us a revealing picture of a question and answer session one day on the riverbank where John was baptizing. "Then came also publicans to be baptized, and said unto him, Master, what shall we do? And he said unto them, Exact no more than that which is appointed you" Luke, Chapter 3.

How truly did the finger of God point out their weak spot as this Spirit-filled prophet answered.

Jesus, in giving His parable of the sower, pointed to the fact that the life which produces the most fruitful harvest is the one that has heard the word with an *honest* heart. He said, "But that on the good ground are they, which in an honest and good heart, having heard the word, keep it, and bring forth fruit with patience" Luke, Chapter 8.

The first deacons of the apostolic church had to be seven men designated as being of *honest* report. (See Acts, Chapter 6.) It doesn't even mention how much they will be able to pledge to the annual budget.

God never lowered His requirements for those who aspire to the Christian walk. "Providing for honest things, not only in the sight of the Lord, but also in the sight of men" 2 Corinthians, Chapter 8.

To the Romans he gave detailed instruction on how to conduct their day-to-day relationships, and thus measure up to God's requirements. "For this cause pay ye tribute also: for they are God's ministers, attending continually upon this very thing. Render therefore to all their dues: tribute to whom tribute is due; custom to whom custom; fear to whom fear; honour to whom honour. Owe no man any thing, but to love one another; for he that loveth another hath fulfilled the law" Romans, Chapter 13.

Christians must watch that they not be snared by the devil in developing the poor pay habits that are on the rise in this easy-credit era. I have been guilty and had to pay a price for it. We must be "good pay" and live a sparkling testimony for Christ's name in this area. "Let us walk honestly . . ." Romans, Chapter 13.

In the epistle to the Hebrews, "Pray for us: for we trust we have a good conscience, in all things willing to live honestly" Hebrews, Chapter 13.

Now we have seen how God views honesty in every matter. God will honor and prosper an honest worker.

We must remember that *our lives* are His display of Christianity at work before the whole world.

18

THE CALDRON'S BREW

Worry and anxiety are from the virus of fear. Fear is not a product of heaven. It is cooked in the pots of hell. It is the opposite of the product of God's Word called FAITH. ". . . faith cometh by hearing, and hearing by the word of God" Romans, Chapter 10.

Fear spurs the sale of alcohol and pills. When man buys fear from the prince of this world his effectiveness freezes. His spirit becomes locked. The frightened child puts his head under the covers. The frightened ostrich buries his head in the sand. The tension-racked man flees to the bottle. Which one is the smartest?

God hates worry in His children, for its presence reveals that we don't really believe His Word—that we doubt His bright provisions. Worry is negative confession. When it rages in our being it can open us up to happenings which otherwise might never occur. Psychiatric researchers have found that 97 percent of the things men worry about never come to pass. Isn't that ironic?

Worry, fear, and anxiety have glutted our mental institutions, hospitals and suicide morgues. Worry is an abomination to God. He wants us to trade in our worries for *His promises.*

Jesus said, "Therefore I say unto you, Take no thought for your life, what ye shall eat, or what ye shall drink; nor yet for your body, what ye shall put on. Is not the life more than meat, and the body than raiment" Matthew, Chapter 6?

The words, *take no thought,* mean, of course, don't worry, don't fret. Kick out anxiety! Let in faith from God's Word.

Jesus said that cares and covetousness smother out the Word in our lives and choke out fruitfulness. They rob us of a serene attitude and stifle our spirit.

"Consider the lilies how they grow: they toil not, they spin not; and yet I say unto you, that Solomon in all his glory was not arrayed like one of these. If then God so clothe the grass, which is to day in the field, and to morrow is cast into the oven; how much more will he clothe you, O ye of little faith? And seek not ye what ye shall eat, or what ye shall drink, neither be ye of doubtful mind. For all these things do the nations of the world seek after: and your Father knoweth that ye have need of these things. But rather seek ye the kingdom of God; and all these things shall be added unto you" Luke, Chapter 12.

". . . the cares of this world, and the deceitfulness of riches, and the lusts of other things entering in, choke the word, and it becometh unfruitful" Mark, Chapter 4.

He warned that it is possible to get so engrossed with earthly cares as to miss out on His return. A horrible thought, but one that is true and now most relevant. It is a time to be sober and with eyes glancing heavenward.

". . . take heed to yourselves, lest at any time your hearts be overcharged with surfeiting, and drunkenness, and cares of this life, and so that day come upon you unawares" Luke, Chapter 21.

God gives us rich counsel on how to avoid Christ-dishonoring worry and discontentment.

"Let your conversation be without covetousness; and be content with such things as ye have: for he hath said, I will never leave thee, nor forsake thee" Hebrews, Chapter 13.

"But godliness with contentment is great gain. And having food and raiment let us be therewith content" 1 Timothy, Chapter 6.

This doesn't mean we aren't to press forward under God to excel in life. It means to work and live as unto Him with all our might, but to cast our worries upon Him. "Casting all your care upon him, for he careth for you" 1 Peter, Chapter 5.

We have a tendency to fear at times what men will do to us. Will we be maligned, sued, hated, harmed, cheated, etc.? Christians ought not to fear men when God says He wants to be our High Tower and the Cleft of the Rock for our protection.

During an important corporate sale some years ago a group of opportunist buyers launched a scheme to try to lower the purchase price they had agreed to pay for the business. Knowing we were sensitive about our business reputation and that we weren't the type that would sue, they commenced a fear assault against us.

They unjustly claimed that we had misrepresented the inventory, even though it had been checked by their auditors and by ours. They threatened public exposure while flailing the air and cursing right in our offices. They sent threatening registered letters through their lawyer. Boy, it was a bit fearful! Prayer finally turned the tide. The Lord said in effect, "Stand your ground. Don't worry about your reputation if you are right before Me." He reminded us that He had been for a season without reputation.

He gave me two Scriptures during the heat of that fierce assault:

". . . we may boldly say, the Lord is my helper, and I will not fear what man shall do unto me" Hebrews, Chapter 13.

". . . Fear them not: for I have delivered them into thine hand; there shall not a man of them stand before thee" Joshua, Chapter 10.

The back of this vicious assault was broken! We never had to raise a hand in our defense thereafter. Yes, God's promises are still relevant in this supersonic age, for He is the same yesterday, today and forever. No wonder He says, "Be careful [or anxious] for nothing; but in every thing by prayer and supplication with thanksgiving let your requests be made known unto God. And the peace of God, which passeth all understanding, shall keep your hearts and minds through Christ Jesus" Philippians, Chapter 4.

That's our Father's answer to tranquilizers!

19

THE TELLERS WERE ANGELS

Generosity is a golden thread that weaves throughout the New Testament. People asked John the Baptist, "What shall *we* do then?" He answered, "He that hath two coats, let him impart to him that hath none; and he that hath meat, let him do likewise" Luke, Chapter 3.

The Lord is saying through the prophet "Don't pile up excess, redundant possessions and wealth." Share these in the Lord's name with the poor. Then God will be able to flow more riches *through* you. It's not easy for Him to find hands that aren't sticky in passing riches to the needy. Jesus cheered on His followers, ". . . freely ye have received, freely give" Matthew, Chapter 10.

Many Christians grumble about the billions for welfare that have exploded our taxes. But *we* are responsible! It's so irritating to us that with the government welfare system it seems better to thousands of people to laze around idle than to take a job.

But God intended that His children be the salt—the preservative. We were meant to light the way and be an example for society. We have relinquished our role in society by our disobedience to God's Word on charity toward the needy. We have grown both callous toward the needy and quick to let Washington do it. When we were children, the family out of work was cheerfully helped. And we took the responsibility ourselves when our parents grew too old to care for themselves.

Today the neighbor out of a job is given a lift to the unemployment office. Big deal! For some parents the help they get from their children is in filling out papers for the old folk's home. Have you ever visited one of these? They aren't God's best—He has no "discards" and He blesses those who still honor their parents.

So often His commandments are followed by a powerful promise of blessings to those who will act on them. They are surefire formulas for godly *prosperity* for us if we do our part. God will never be outdone. "Give, and it shall be given unto you; good measure, pressed down, and shaken together, and running over, shall men give into your bosom. For with the same measure that ye mete withal it shall be measured to you again" Luke, Chapter 6.

Transfer your assets to heaven while there is still time. The windows are always open and the tellers may be angels.

It's not too hard for us to be generous to nice Christian friends. But there is one very difficult injunction from the Lord! "Therefore if thine enemy hunger, feed him; if he thirst, give him drink: for in so doing thou shalt heap coals of fire on his head" Romans, Chapter 12.

But, Lord, you couldn't mean *him* could you?

Yes, you read it right! I suspect there's a special blessing from God for obedience to this startling admonition. After all, Jesus gave Himself for His enemies as well as His friends.

A further breathtaking word from God on the subject of generosity and good works is this: "Let brotherly love continue. Be not forgetful to entertain strangers: for thereby some have entertained angels unawares" Hebrews, Chapter 13.

I wouldn't like to miss out on the possibility of entertaining a heavenly guest, would you? You may have already! How did you treat him? Did you send him away because he looked so unimportant? Because you were too busy? Because he interrupted your television program?

Then Jesus said, that when you visit the sick, feed the hungry, clothe the naked, minister to those in prison, "Ye have done it unto me" Matthew, Chapter 25.

Isn't it a paradox that in the time of the world's greatest material prosperity this bureaucratic charity had to come into being? God's children neglected His injunction to share with the needy so finally the government had to step in. No wonder it is a program fraught with confusion and empty of appreciation. Impersonal government welfare is taken for granted and often taken advantage of. *It isn't being done in God's name,* as He instructed us to do it, and so the system is critically flawed.

"And whosoever shall give to drink unto one of these little ones a cup of cold water only in the name of a disciple, verily I say unto you, he shall in no wise lose his reward" Matthew, Chapter 10.

20

PERILS OF GOLD

The basic issue isn't how much or how few things we own, but whether or not they are beginning to dominate our lives. Can we survive in a climate of affluence still thankful to God or do we start clutching for more? Is our business and our prosperity becoming an idol?

Paul wrote to Timothy about the perils of affluence. This is why we see so many miserable rich, with their lives entangled: "But they that will be rich fall into temptation and a snare, and into many foolish and hurtful lusts, which drown men in destruction and perdition. For the love of money is the root of all evil: which while some coveted after, they have erred from the faith, and pierced themselves through with many sorrows" 1 Timothy, Chapter 6.

Note again, "the love of money" is the evil root. Some who have no money lust for it more than the rich. Criminals lust for unearned money.

J. B. Phillips says, that they who crave to be rich fall into trouble! "For loving money leads into all kinds of evil . . ." 1 Timothy, Chapter 6 (PHILLIPS). The Lord seems to be counseling the rich throughout the Bible. He must have loved them to do so.

"Charge them that are rich in this world, that they be not highminded, nor trust in uncertain riches, but in the living God, who giveth us richly all things to enjoy; They that do good, that they be rich in good works, ready to redistribute, willing to communicate; Laying up in store for themselves a good foundation against the time to come, that they may lay hold on eternal life" Chapter 6.

Prosperity seems to be sought by everybody, but it is a state fraught with great spiritual hazards. It takes a committed strong believer to remain upright under conditions of great wealth. Even then it is perilous.

It was Jesus who made the observation, ". . . a rich man will find it very difficult to enter the kingdom of Heaven" Matthew, Chapter 19 (PHILLIPS).

In Paul's letter to Timothy we read of men whose thinking is so twisted that they still teach that earthly prosperity is a mark of righteousness. A study of the secret lives of many rich people would shatter this illusion. "Perverse disputings of men of corrupt minds, and destitute of the truth, supposing that gain is godliness; and from such withdraw thyself. But godliness with contentment is great gain" 1 Timothy, Chapter 6.

In a recently published book the writer states that "to suppose that unruffled seas and blue skies are a token of divine approval is the cruel conceit of those with whom all things go well."

HOW TO GIVE

Give willingly and in proportion to your holdings:

"For if there be first a willing mind, it is accepted according to that a man hath, and not according to that he hath not. For I mean not that other men be eased, and ye burdened: But by an equality, that now at this time your abundance may be a supply for their want, that their abundance also may be a supply for your want: that there may be equality: As it is written, He that had gathered much had nothing over; and he that had gathered little had no lack" 2 Corinthians, Chapter 8.

"Then the people rejoiced, for that they offered willingly, because with perfect heart they offered willingly to the Lord and David the king also rejoiced with great joy" 1 Chronicles, Chapter 29.

Give cheerfully and generously:

"But this I say, He which soweth sparingly shall reap also sparingly; and he which soweth bountifully shall reap also bountifully. Every man according as he purposeth in his heart, so let him give; not grudgingly, or of necessity: for God loveth a cheerful giver. And God is able to make all grace abound toward you; that ye, always having all sufficiency in all things, may abound to every good work. (As it is written, He hath dispersed abroad; he hath given to the poor: his righteousness remaineth for ever. Now he that ministereth seed to the sower both minister bread for your food, and multiply your seed sown, and increase the fruits of your righteousness;) Being enriched in every thing to all bountifulness, which causeth through us thanksgiving to God" 2 Corinthians, Chapter 9.

It is crystal clear what we must do to receive back from God in abundance. Giving in His name is a prerequisite. Note that our money is to be shared generously with *every good work*. Give freely to good ministries if you want to be a channel for God's prosperity. Be in much prayer as to *which* works you are to give to. Pray earnestly on this matter of which ministries God would have you fund. Don't get in a rut. Generously support your local church, but also give to other fruitful ministries—ones that are gathering a big harvest. Both the *amount* and the *where* are important to God. This exciting Scripture has been a fountainhead for thousands of prosperous Christians.

Give in support of those who labor in God's vineyard:

"For the scripture saith, Thou shalt not muzzle the ox that treadeth out the corn. And, The labourer is worthy of his reward" 1 Timothy, Chapter 5.

It is most important that we not just bask under ministry and blessing from a servant of God while neglecting monetary support for his work. We aren't to judge his present affluence either. If he has ministered—reward him. God will bless you for your obedience and if he has more than he needs the Lord will show him what to do with it.

Many enjoy radio, TV and direct ministries month after month, while carelessly neglecting their support. We aren't to take these ministries for granted. *All* of God's oxen are to be fed and none muzzled by us. We must learn to more effectively *worship God with our pocketbooks*. Especially since it's near the day of His return.

"Even so hath the Lord ordained that they which preach the gospel should live of the gospel" 1 Corinthians, Chapter 9.

Beloved, let's begin to give in such a spirit of generosity that God can say this about us, ". . . we must tell you about the grace that God has given to the Macedonian churches. Somehow, in most difficult circumstances, their joy, and the fact of their being down to their last penny themselves, produced a magnificent concern for other people. I can guarantee that they were willing to give to the limit of their means, yes and beyond their means, without the slightest urging from me or anyone else. In fact they simply begged us to accept their gifts . . ." 2 Corinthians, Chapter 8 (PHILLIPS).

Give regularly and systematically:

Even in our New Testament age God asks the same financial worship *disciplines* if we seek prosperity of our spirit and pocketbook. Haphazard, intermittent, impulsive giving are contrary to God's success plans. He says pointedly, "Upon the first day of the week let every one of you lay by him in store, as God hath prospered him, that there be no gatherings when I come" 1 Corinthians, Chapter 16.

A friend of mine is a supermarket owner in Montana. He goes his Lord one better! He thanks the Lord at the end of every single day for the business he has done and then tithes *daily*. God has incredibly prospered him since he started this.

You know, there's no room for complacent self-righteousness on the part of anyone. Neither is there in the household of faith any place for pride. God detests the pride of life that stalks every human.

We are to grow together unto a holy temple in the Lord. Each day that we live should move us toward another spiritual plateau. There can be no standing still, no marking time, and no parking at any spiritual level. We never fully attain here. We must in all matters *press on* toward that mark of the high calling! Only the Word of God is to remain unchanging and unchanged. May we enthusiastically allow our lives to be shaped by His precepts, and remain eagerly teachable.

> Then shall all conflict cease, all fetters fall,
> And Christ shall be our Peace, our All in all.

Too often we respond to habit in our giving. Often mindlessly reacting to an offering plate. The amounts given aren't even as important as our attitude of giving. He looks on our heart as we give rather than just operating His adding machine.

Pray before you feel that offering basket in your hand. Try telling Him that you aren't giving in a routine automatic way anymore, but as a conscious *act of praise*. As thanksgiving for His love, mercy, goodness and bounty to you. Confess with your mouth that every dollar you have is from Him and that you are excited about giving to Him.

But don't ever hesitate to tell God the *truth* as to how you feel about giving or anything else. We can freely say, without shame, "Lord, I don't honestly like to give my money today. I need every dollar of this. We're short right now. Forgive me for not really wanting to do this. I confess this is an attitude of unbelief, for you said you would always take care of us. So today I'm giving this as a sacrifice. So, Lord, receive this gift for I know that I can't afford not to give."

Remember the man who said to Jesus, ". . . I believe; help thou mine unbelief" Mark, Chapter 9. He was saying, "I believe you with my spirit, but with my logical mind it's hard. Jesus rewarded the honest transparency and his confession. So will it be as we learn to pray honestly and to give largely. Then—watch things begin to happen in your life!

There is a pattern. The hand of God is moved by *giving*. Do we long for Divine intervention in our life? After Abraham *gave* Isaac he was made the father of many nations. When the widow of Zarephath *gave* the last of her food to God's prophet, it multiplied and she lived. When the harlot *gave* refuge, she received salvation! When Hannah *gave* her unborn son, he became the greatest priest in Israel's history. When David *gave* for the temple building, his personal wealth grew. When the farmer *gave* his threshing floor for the ark, he was prospered. When Moses *gave* his rod, it was charged with life and power.

It still is His pattern in our supersonic age. The LeTourneaus, Penneys, DeMosses, Kresges, Johnsons, Stones, Shakarians and scores of others have proven God by giving, and He has responded in our modern day with a heavenly avalanche—". . . pressed down, and shaken together, and running over . . ." Luke, Chapter 6.

21

HEAVENLY POTPOURRI

PEACE AND BLESSINGS

"Great peace have they which love thy law: and nothing shall offend them" Psalms, Chapter 119.

"The blessing of the Lord, it maketh rich, and he addeth no sorrow with it" Proverbs, Chapter 10.

"Thou wilt keep him in perfect peace, whose mind is stayed on thee: because he trusteth in thee" Isaiah, Chapter 26.

"O that thou hadst hearkened to my commandments! then had thy peace been as a river, and thy righteousness as the waves of the sea" Chapter 48.

"Peace I leave with you, my peace I give unto you: not as the world giveth, give I unto you. Let not your heart be troubled, neither let it be afraid" John, Chapter 14.

"Blessed be the God and Father of our Lord Jesus Christ, who hath blessed us with all spiritual blessings in heavenly places in Christ" Ephesians, Chapter 1.

HOW TO BUY A CURSE

"Behold, I set before you this day a blessing and a curse; A blessing, if ye obey the commandments of the Lord your God . . . And a curse, if ye will not obey the commandments of the Lord your God . . ." Deuteronomy, Chapter 11.

". . . I have set before you life and death, blessing and cursing: therefore choose life . . ." Chapter 30.

"The curse of the Lord is in the house of the wicked . . ." Proverbs, Chapter 3.

"I am the vine, ye are the branches . . . if a man abide not in me, he is cast forth as a branch, and is withered; and men

gather them, and cast them into the fire, and they are burned"
John, Chapter 15.

In Genesis, Chapter 12, God wrote to us concerning the Jew:
"And I will bless them that bless thee, and curse him that curseth
thee . . ." It's a law that's still in full force today.

We might even say, *especially* today for since the Six-Day War,
Jerusalem is no longer trodden down by the Gentiles. God said
He would (at that time) begin to lift the spiritual slumber from
the Jews. Today we see exciting evidence that He is doing that.
Suddenly more Jews are finding Christ as their Messiah than in
past centuries.

Then too, we musn't inadvertently curse the Jews. It's time to
love them! As Gentiles we have felt a gulf, a fear, an ignorance
and an incapability in approaching Jews about Jesus.

We are now faced with a fabulous new opportunity to be
blessed by turning again "to the Jew first." The time has fully
come when their slumber is lifting and we can partake of God's
blessing by now blessing the Jews. God's alarm clock is now
ringing for them.

Let's begin to approach them as *people*. Why, we've almost
forgotten they're just people too. Tell them in your own way about
their Messiah. Tell them of the power of God that is now being
shed abroad on all people just as their own prophets wrote about.
And let's start giving generously to works that are evangelizing
among the Jews.

Yes, bless the Jews and God will bless you!

FROM A WEALTHY FATHER

"This book of the law shall not depart out of thy mouth; but
thou shalt meditate therein day and night, that thou mayest observe
to do according to all that is written therein: for then thou shalt
make thy way prosperous, and then thou shalt have good success"
Joshua, Chapter 1.

"Therefore the Lord hath recompensed me according to my
righteousness; according to my cleanness in his eye sight" 2
Samuel, Chapter 29.

". . . the Lord will give grace and glory: no good thing will
he withhold from them that walk uprightly" Psalms, Chapter 84.

"The law of thy mouth is better unto me than thousands of gold and silver" Chapter 119.

"Honour the Lord with thy substance, and with the firstfruits of all thine increase: So shall thy barns be filled with plenty, and thy presses shall burst out with new wine" Proverbs, Chapter 3.

"He that trusteth in his riches shall fall . . ." Chapter 11.

"There is that maketh himself rich, yet hath nothing: there is that maketh himself poor, yet hath great riches" Chapter 13.

"Labour not to be rich: cease from thine own wisdom . . . for riches certainly make themselves wings; they fly away as an eagle toward heaven" Chapter 23.

"[Be] Not slothful in business; fervent in spirit; serving the Lord" Romans, Chapter 12.

"Charge them that are rich in this world, that they be not highminded, nor trust in uncertain riches, but in the living God, who giveth us richly all things to enjoy" 1 Timothy, Chapter 6.

"Every good gift and every perfect gift is from above, and cometh down from the Father of lights . . ." James, Chapter 1.

PROFITABLE WELFARE

"The liberal soul shall be made fat: and he that watereth shall be watered also himself" Proverbs, Chapter 11.

"He that hath pity upon the poor lendeth unto the Lord; and that which he hath given will he pay him again" Chapter 19.

"He that hath a bountiful eye shall be blessed; for he giveth of his bread to the poor" Chapter 22.

"He that giveth unto the poor shall not lack . . ." Chapter 28.

". . . do good, and lend, hoping for nothing again; and your reward shall be great, and ye shall be the children of the Highest . . . Be ye therefore merciful, as your Father also is merciful" Luke, Chapter 6.

We are today treating too many needy people the way most treated the poor fellow in the story of the Good Samaritan. The Bible teaches that it isn't enough for us to just pray for one in need. It won't cut any ice with God for us to say, "God bless you, we'll be praying for your needs." We read in James, Chapter 2, "If a brother or sister be naked, and destitute of daily food, And one of you say unto them, Depart in peace, be ye warmed and filled; notwithstanding ye give them not those things which are needful to the body; what doth it profit?"

Someone has said, "What we have is God's gift to us; what we do with it is our gift to Him."

INTEGRITY

"These are the things that ye shall do; Speak ye every man the truth . . . and love no false oath: for all these are things that I hate, saith the Lord" Zechariah, Chapter 8.

"The man who can be trusted in little things can be trusted also in great; and the man who is dishonest in little things is dishonest also in great things. . . . If you have proved untrustworthy with what belongs to another, who will give you what is your own" Luke, Chapter 16 (NEB)?

"Provide things honest in the sight of all men" Romans, Chapter 12.

"Let us walk honestly . . ." Chapter 13.

INDOLENCE—POVERTY—WANT

"Go to the ant, thou sluggard; consider her ways, and be wise: Which . . . provideth her meat in the summer, and gathereth her food in the harvest. How long wilt thou sleep, O sluggard? when wilt thou arise out of thy sleep? Yet a little sleep, a little slumber, a little folding of the hands to sleep: So shall thy poverty come as one that travelleth, and thy want as an armed man" Proverbs, Chapter 6.

"He becometh poor that dealeth with a slack hand . . ." Chapter 10.

". . . he that sleepeth in harvest is a son that causeth shame" Chapter 10.

"The sluggard will not plow by reason of the cold; therefore shall he beg in harvest, and have nothing" Chapter 20.

"The desire of the slothful killeth him; for his hands refuse to labour" Chapter 21.

But God says, "the sleep of a labouring man is sweet . . ." Ecclesiastes, Chapter 5.

DISHONESTY—DECEIT

These six things doth the Lord hate: yea, seven are an abomination unto him: A proud look, a lying tongue, and hands that shed innocent blood, An heart that deviseth wicked imaginations, feet that be swift in running to mischief, A false witness that speaketh lies, and he that soweth discord among brethren" Proverbs, Chapter 6.

"A false balance is abomination to the Lord: but a just weight is his delight" Chapter 11.

"But [we] have renounced the hidden things of dishonesty, not walking in craftiness, nor handling the word of God deceitfully; but by manifestation of the truth commending ourselves to every man's conscience in the sight of God" 2 Corinthians, Chapter 4.

THE SHADOW OF THE WING

"The Lord is my rock, and my fortress, and my deliverer; my God, my strength, in whom I will trust . . ." Psalms, Chapter 18.

"Some trust in chariots, and some in horses: but we will remember the name of the Lord our God" Chapter 20.

"For in the time of trouble he shall hide me in his pavilion: in the secret of his tabernacle shall he hide me; he shall set me up upon a rock" Chapter 27.

"Oh how great is thy goodness, which thou hast laid up for them that fear thee; which thou hast wrought for them that trust in thee before the sons of men! Thou shalt hide them in the secret of thy presence from the pride of man: thou shalt keep them secretly in the pavilion from the strife of tongues" Chapter 31.

"Trust in the Lord and do good; so shalt thou dwell in the land, and verily thou shalt be fed" Chapter 37.

"He shall cover thee with his feathers, and under his wings shalt thou trust: his truth shall be thy shield and buckler" Chapter 91.

"My help cometh from the Lord, which made heaven and earth. He will not suffer thy foot to be moved . . ." Chapter 121.

"He will not suffer thy foot to be moved: he that keepeth thee will not slumber" Chapter 121.

"Trust in the Lord with all thine heart; and lean not unto thine own understanding. In all thy ways acknowledge him, and he shall direct thy paths," Proverbs, Chapter 3.

"The name of the Lord is a strong tower: the righteous runneth into it, and is safe" Chapter 18.

"Thou wilt keep him in perfect peace, whose mind is stayed on thee: because he trusteth in thee" Isaiah, Chapter 26.

"The Lord is good, a strong hold in the day of trouble; and he knoweth them that trust in him" Nahum, Chapter 1.

". . . whosoever heareth these sayings of mine, and doeth them, I will liken him unto a wise man, which built his house upon a rock: And the rain descended, and the floods came, and the winds blew, and beat upon that house; and it fell not: for it was founded upon a rock" Matthew, Chapter 7.

"My sheep hear my voice, and I know them, and they follow me: And I give unto them eternal life; and they shall never perish, neither shall any man pluck them out of my hand. My Father, which gave them to me, is greater than all; and no man is able to pluck them out of my Father's hand" John, Chapter 10.

May we emulate Cornelius the godly centurion to whom an angel spoke these words, ". . . Thy prayers and thine alms are come up for a memorial before God" Acts, Chapter 10.

THE BLUEPRINT

It may have come as a surprise to many that the Bible says: ". . . Let the Lord be magnified, which hath pleasure in the prosperity of his servant" Psalms, Chapter 35.

Prosperity is the will of God for the believer. He loves to heal cancer of the body, but many of us haven't before realized that He is ready to heal cancer of the pocketbook. But for every blessing He makes available, there is a condition to be met. Christians should know that every promise is conditional. We don't get His blessings automatically, we must first meet the condition . . . and *then* God fulfills His divine promise to us.

WHAT ARE THE CONDITIONS FOR PROSPERITY?

Deuteronomy, Chapter 29: Keep God's Word.

2 Chronicles, Chapter 20: Believe in the Lord, and believe His prophets.

2 Chronicles, Chapter 26: Seek the Lord.

Psalms, Chapter 1: Be righteous.

Malachi, Chapter 3: Give tithes and offerings.

Matthew, Chapter 6: Put God first.

Luke, Chapter 6: Give first . . . before you receive.

2 Corinthians, Chapter 9: Give generously.

1 Chronicles, Chapter 29: Give enthusiastically.

Hebrews, Chapter 6: Then expect His blessings.

These will give an insight into God's will and purpose for mankind. If you are right with God—if you live right, think right, act right, put the right things uppermost in your heart and mind, seek first things first—then God will bless you, prosper you, and keep you in health.

Are you conforming to God's purposes? Are you personally involved in reaping the world harvest? Are you laboring and living to further the Kingdom of God? Are you enthusiastic in your giving to sustain His works? Are you concerned about these things . . . which are of great concern to God? If you can answer Yes to these questions, then the balances can swing in your favor concerning your personal needs. Jesus said: "But seek ye first the kingdom of God, and his righteousness; and all these things shall be added unto you" [food, clothing, shelter etc.] Matthew, Chapter 6. Yes, one of his principal names is actually Jehovah—Jireh (the Lord, our Provider). It is He who shouts, "If ye be willing and obedient, ye shall eat the good of the land" Isaiah, Chapter 1. Don't say, "I can't do it. It's too hard." For you can do all things through Christ. If you falter, ask forgiveness and press on expectantly.

Yes, from Genesis through Revelation, the Bible, God's Treasure Map, charts prosperity for His own! Your Heavenly Father longs to share His inexhaustible riches with you starting today!